The Allostatic Architecture

Building Better Health

Len Webb

Chapter 1: Understanding Allostasis and Health

Defining Allostasis Beyond Homeostasis

Maintaining life requires far more than simple equilibrium - it demands an intricate dance of adaptation and anticipation. While homeostasis describes the body's tendency to maintain stable internal conditions, allostasis represents a more sophisticated and dynamic model of how living organisms truly function and thrive in an ever-changing world.

The concept of allostasis emerged when researchers realized that optimal biological function isn't about maintaining rigid set points, but rather about flexibly adjusting multiple parameters in anticipation of challenges. Think of a runner preparing for a race - their body begins making adjustments to heart rate, blood pressure, and energy metabolism well before the starting gun fires. This predictive adaptation exemplifies allostasis in action.

Unlike homeostasis, which operates like a simple thermostat maintaining a fixed temperature, allostasis functions more like an intelligent climate control system that considers multiple variables and future needs. It acknowledges that what's "optimal" varies based on context - a heart rate that's appropriate during exercise would be concerning at rest. This dynamic regulation occurs through complex networks of neural, endocrine, and immune processes working in concert.

The brilliance of allostasis lies in its anticipatory nature. Rather than waiting to react to disruptions, allostatic systems prepare the body for predicted challenges. During acute stress, this might mean mobilizing energy reserves, increasing alertness, and enhancing immune function - all coordinated responses that help navigate threatening situations. These adaptations occur through intricate feedback loops involving the hypothalamus, pituitary gland, and adrenal glands, among other systems.

Consider how the body prepares for physical activity. Blood pressure and heart rate increase, muscles receive enhanced blood flow, and energy stores are mobilized - all before significant exertion begins. This orchestrated response demonstrates how allostatic regulation extends beyond simple homeostatic balance to create optimal conditions for anticipated demands.

The temporal aspect of allostasis is crucial. While homeostatic systems operate primarily in the present moment, allostatic regulation considers past experiences and future needs. This temporal integration allows for learning and adaptation based on previous challenges while preparing for potential future demands. A person who regularly exercises develops not just stronger muscles, but more efficient allostatic responses to physical stress.

Understanding allostasis reveals why the same physiological response can be either adaptive or harmful depending on context and duration. Short-term stress responses are generally beneficial, preparing the body for challenge and enhancing performance. However, when these responses become chronic or excessive, they can lead to wear and tear on biological systems - a phenomenon known as allostatic load.

The complexity of allostatic regulation becomes apparent when examining how different systems interact. Stress hormones don't just affect heart rate and blood pressure; they influence immune function, digestion, reproduction, and cognitive performance. This interconnectedness explains why chronic stress can impact seemingly unrelated aspects of health, from susceptibility to infections to memory formation.

Modern life presents unique challenges to our allostatic systems. Our bodies evolved to handle acute physical threats, but today's chronic psychological stressors - like work deadlines or financial worries - can trigger the same physiological responses. Without appropriate recovery periods, these persistent adaptations can become maladaptive.

The implications of allostasis extend beyond individual health. Environmental factors, social relationships, and early life experiences all influence allostatic regulation. This broader perspective helps explain how socioeconomic conditions and chronic stress can lead to health disparities across populations.

Recognizing allostasis as the fundamental principle of biological regulation transforms our approach to health and wellness. Instead of focusing solely on maintaining stable conditions, we must consider how to support adaptive capacity and resilience. This might involve strategies to enhance recovery between challenges, reduce unnecessary stressors, and strengthen the body's predictive abilities.

The shift from homeostasis to allostasis represents more than a theoretical advancement - it provides a framework for understanding how living organisms actually maintain health in a dynamic environment. This understanding opens new avenues for promoting wellness and preventing disease by supporting the body's natural adaptive capabilities rather than simply treating symptoms when balance is disrupted.

The Bodys Dynamic Equilibrium

Life pulses with constant change, yet maintains a remarkable order through dynamic equilibrium - a delicate balancing act that keeps us functioning through ever-shifting conditions. Within every cell, tissue, and organ system, countless processes work in concert to maintain this intricate dance of stability and adaptation.

The human body operates like a sophisticated orchestra, where each instrument must play its part precisely while remaining responsive to the overall composition. This dynamic equilibrium involves multiple systems working simultaneously across different time scales. Blood pressure adjusts with each heartbeat, while hormones fluctuate throughout the day, and bone density changes over months and years.

Consider the complexity of blood glucose regulation. When we eat, insulin helps cells absorb glucose from the bloodstream, while glucagon releases stored energy when glucose levels fall. This isn't a simple on-off switch, but rather a nuanced interplay responding to numerous factors - recent meals, physical activity, stress levels, and even time of day. The pancreas must constantly adjust its hormone production to maintain optimal blood sugar levels while anticipating upcoming needs.

Temperature regulation provides another striking example of dynamic equilibrium. The body maintains its core temperature through an intricate network of sensors, feedback loops, and responses. When we exercise, blood vessels dilate near the skin's surface to release heat, sweat glands activate, and breathing rate increases. Conversely, in cold conditions, blood vessels constrict, muscles shiver, and metabolism adjusts - all without conscious control.

The cardiovascular system demonstrates remarkable adaptability in maintaining dynamic equilibrium. Heart rate and blood pressure constantly adjust to meet changing demands, influenced by posture, emotion, activity level, and environmental conditions. Standing up from a lying position triggers immediate cardiovascular adjustments to maintain blood flow to the brain, while emotional stress can rapidly increase heart rate and blood pressure in preparation for action.

Sleep-wake cycles represent a larger-scale example of dynamic equilibrium. Rather than maintaining constant alertness, the body cycles through different states of consciousness, each serving essential functions for physical and mental health. These cycles respond to both internal cues, like accumulated sleep pressure, and external signals, such as light exposure and social schedules.

The immune system maintains its own dynamic equilibrium, constantly patrolling for threats while avoiding overreaction to harmless stimuli. This balance requires sophisticated recognition mechanisms and carefully calibrated responses. Too weak a response leaves us vulnerable to infection, while too strong a response can trigger autoimmune conditions or chronic inflammation.

Muscle tissue exemplifies dynamic equilibrium through its constant process of breakdown and rebuilding. Physical activity causes micro-damage to muscle fibers, triggering repair processes that ultimately strengthen the tissue. This ongoing cycle of stress and recovery allows for adaptation to changing demands while maintaining functional stability.

The digestive system demonstrates dynamic equilibrium through its rhythmic contractions and precise timing of enzyme release. It must coordinate the breakdown of various nutrients while maintaining appropriate pH levels and protecting against harmful substances. This complex choreography adjusts to different types and quantities of food while maintaining optimal absorption of nutrients.

Mental and emotional states also exist in dynamic equilibrium, fluctuating naturally while generally maintaining stability over time. Mood, attention, and cognitive performance all vary throughout the day, influenced by circadian rhythms, energy levels, and environmental demands. This natural variation allows for appropriate responses to different situations while preventing extreme or prolonged emotional states.

Hormonal systems exemplify the interconnected nature of dynamic equilibrium. The hypothalamic-pituitary axis coordinates multiple hormone cascades that influence everything from growth and metabolism to stress response and reproduction. These systems must constantly adjust to maintain optimal function while responding to both internal and external changes.

Understanding dynamic equilibrium reveals why rigid approaches to health often fail. The body doesn't seek absolute stability but rather maintains function through constant adjustment and adaptation. This perspective suggests that health interventions should focus on supporting these natural regulatory processes rather than forcing artificial stability.

The concept of dynamic equilibrium extends beyond individual systems to encompass the entire organism's relationship with its environment. Our bodies constantly interact with and adapt to changing external conditions - physical, social, and environmental factors all influence our internal state. This ongoing dialogue between internal and external forces shapes our health and resilience over time.

Stress Response Systems

Our bodies possess an intricate network of stress response systems that have evolved over millions of years to protect and preserve life in the face of challenges. These sophisticated mechanisms activate within milliseconds of perceiving a threat, orchestrating a complex cascade of physiological and behavioral changes that prepare us for action.

The immediate stress response begins in the amygdala, the brain's emotional processing center, which rapidly assesses potential threats and triggers the hypothalamus to initiate the fight-or-flight response. Within seconds, the sympathetic nervous system springs into action, releasing epinephrine and norepinephrine throughout the body. Heart rate accelerates, breathing quickens, and blood flow redirects to essential muscles and organs.

Simultaneously, the hypothalamic-pituitary-adrenal (HPA) axis activates, releasing corticotropin-releasing hormone (CRH), which triggers the production of adrenocorticotropic hormone (ACTH) from the pituitary gland. This hormonal cascade culminates in the release of cortisol from the adrenal glands, producing widespread effects throughout the body that can last for hours or even days.

Beyond these primary stress response systems, secondary mechanisms engage to support the body's adaptive efforts. The immune system modifies its activity, temporarily enhancing certain functions while suppressing others. Digestive processes slow down, reproductive functions take a back seat, and energy stores mobilize to provide readily available fuel for action.

The complexity of stress response systems becomes apparent when examining their temporal dynamics. Some responses, like the sympathetic nervous system activation, occur almost instantly and are relatively short-lived. Others, such as cortisol release and immune system modifications, develop more gradually and can persist for extended periods. This layered response ensures both immediate survival and longer-term adaptation to challenging conditions.

What makes these systems particularly remarkable is their ability to calibrate their response based on the nature and intensity of the stressor. A minor challenge might trigger a modest cortisol increase, while a severe threat elicits a full-blown stress response. This gradated response helps conserve energy and prevents unnecessary wear and tear on the body.

The recovery phase of the stress response is equally sophisticated. The parasympathetic nervous system, often called the "rest and digest" system, works to restore balance once the threat has passed. Heart rate slows, breathing deepens, and digestive function resumes. This recovery period is crucial for preventing the accumulation of stress-related damage and maintaining long-term health.

Modern life presents unique challenges to our stress response systems. While these mechanisms evolved to handle acute physical threats, today they frequently activate in response to psychological stressors - work deadlines, financial worries, or relationship conflicts. These challenges often persist for extended periods, preventing complete recovery between stress episodes.

The social dimension of stress response systems adds another layer of complexity. Human beings are inherently social creatures, and our stress responses are heavily influenced by our relationships and social environment. Supportive social connections can buffer stress responses, while social isolation or conflict can amplify them.

Environmental factors significantly impact stress response function. Exposure to natural light, physical activity levels, and dietary patterns all influence how effectively these systems operate. Regular exercise, for instance, helps maintain appropriate stress responsiveness while promoting efficient recovery. Proper nutrition provides the building blocks necessary for stress hormone production and cellular repair.

Sleep plays a crucial role in maintaining healthy stress response systems. During sleep, stress hormone levels naturally decline, allowing for tissue repair and recovery. Disrupted sleep patterns can impair this essential restoration process, leading to dysregulated stress responses and increased vulnerability to health problems.

Understanding these systems reveals why chronic stress can have such widespread effects on health. When stress responses remain activated for extended periods, they can contribute to inflammation, immune dysfunction, metabolic disturbances, and accelerated aging. However, this same understanding also points to potential interventions for supporting healthy stress response function.

The plasticity of stress response systems offers hope for improvement through targeted interventions. Regular physical activity, stress management practices, adequate sleep, and proper nutrition can all help optimize these systems' function. Even chronic stress patterns can be modified through consistent attention to lifestyle factors and stress management techniques.

Recognizing the complexity and sophistication of our stress response systems helps us appreciate their vital role in maintaining health while understanding the importance of supporting their proper function. These systems don't just help us survive immediate threats - they shape our resilience, adaptability, and long-term well-being.

Adaptive vs Maladaptive Responses

Biological responses to stress and challenge exist on a spectrum, where the line between helpful and harmful often depends on context, timing, and intensity. What makes a response adaptive in one situation may become maladaptive in another, creating a complex interplay between protection and potential damage.

Adaptive responses typically enhance survival and functioning in the face of challenges. When encountering a physical threat, the rapid increase in heart rate, blood pressure, and muscle tension prepares the body for action. The heightened alertness and focused attention help process environmental information quickly and make split-second decisions. These immediate physiological changes represent perfectly adaptive responses that have evolved over millions of years.

However, these same responses can become maladaptive when activated chronically or in inappropriate contexts. Consider a person experiencing persistent work-related stress. The continued elevation of stress hormones, initially meant to mobilize energy for immediate action, can lead to disrupted sleep, impaired digestion, and weakened immune function. What began as an adaptive response becomes maladaptive through its persistence and intensity.

The immune system provides another clear example of this duality. An acute inflammatory response helps fight infection and repair tissue damage - a crucial adaptive response. Yet chronic inflammation, often triggered by persistent stress or environmental factors, can damage healthy tissue and contribute to numerous diseases. The very mechanisms that protect us can, when dysregulated, become sources of harm.

Learning and memory processes demonstrate similar patterns. The enhanced memory formation during moderately stressful events helps us remember important information and avoid future dangers. However, severe or chronic stress can impair memory function and cognitive flexibility, transforming an adaptive mechanism into a maladaptive one.

Behavioral responses follow comparable patterns. Short-term avoidance of threatening situations can be adaptive, allowing time for preparation or recovery. Yet when avoidance becomes a habitual response to manageable challenges, it limits personal growth and creates additional problems. The key lies in distinguishing between situations where avoidance serves a protective function and those where it hinders adaptation.

Sleep changes illustrate this adaptive-maladaptive continuum. Temporary sleep disruption during times of danger or important deadlines can be adaptive, allowing for necessary vigilance or task completion. However, chronic sleep disturbance, often triggered by persistent worry or irregular schedules, becomes maladaptive, impairing cognitive function and physical health.

The metabolic system demonstrates similar dynamics. The mobilization of energy resources during stress provides crucial fuel for immediate challenges. Yet chronic activation of these pathways can lead to insulin resistance, weight gain, and metabolic dysfunction. What serves as an adaptive energy response in acute situations becomes maladaptive when persistently activated.

Social behavior also reflects this pattern. Increased vigilance and caution in new social situations can be adaptive, protecting against potential threats. However, excessive social anxiety or isolation represents a maladaptive response that creates additional problems and limits opportunities for support and connection.

Understanding the transition from adaptive to maladaptive responses reveals the importance of context and recovery periods. Most adaptive responses become maladaptive primarily when they persist beyond their useful duration or occur in inappropriate situations. Regular recovery periods allow biological systems to reset and maintain their adaptive capacity.

Environmental factors play a crucial role in determining whether responses remain adaptive or become maladaptive. Supportive environments that provide adequate resources and recovery opportunities help maintain adaptive responses. Challenging environments that create persistent demands without sufficient support increase the risk of maladaptive patterns.

The development of adaptive versus maladaptive responses often begins early in life. Early experiences shape how biological systems respond to challenges, influencing whether these responses remain flexible and appropriate or become rigid and harmful. This developmental perspective helps explain why similar stressors can produce different outcomes in different individuals.

Individual differences in temperament and genetic factors also influence the balance between adaptive and maladaptive responses. Some people naturally maintain more flexible and appropriate responses to challenges, while others more readily develop maladaptive patterns. Recognition of these individual differences helps inform personalized approaches to maintaining healthy adaptive responses.

The good news lies in the plasticity of these response systems. Through conscious effort and appropriate support, maladaptive patterns can often be shifted back toward more adaptive responses. This might involve learning new coping strategies, modifying environmental conditions, or gradually exposing oneself to challenges in manageable ways.

Success in maintaining healthy function depends largely on recognizing and supporting adaptive responses while preventing or modifying maladaptive ones. This requires attention to both individual and environmental factors, creating conditions that promote resilience while providing adequate opportunities for recovery and restoration.

The Cost of Adaptation Allostatic Load

Each adaptation to life's challenges carries a biological price tag, accumulating over time in what scientists call allostatic load. Like a car driven hard without proper maintenance, our bodies can wear down under the constant demand to adapt to stressors, leading to accelerated aging and increased disease risk.

The concept of allostatic load represents the cumulative burden of adaptations to stress over time. When we face a challenge, multiple biological systems activate to help us cope - our heart rate increases, stress hormones surge, and immune function adjusts. While these responses are essential for survival, they exact a toll on our bodies, particularly when activated frequently or for extended periods.

Think of allostatic load as a bank account where stress responses create withdrawals. Regular recovery periods allow for deposits back into this account, but when withdrawals consistently exceed deposits, we begin running a biological deficit. This deficit manifests in various ways, from cellular damage to systemic dysfunction.

The cardiovascular system often bears the earliest signs of accumulated allostatic load. Repeated stress responses can lead to chronic elevation of blood pressure, increased heart rate variability, and accelerated atherosclerosis. These changes may initially be subtle but compound over time, increasing the risk of heart disease and stroke.

The immune system similarly shows the effects of mounting allostatic load. Chronic activation of stress responses can suppress immune function, making us more vulnerable to infections while simultaneously promoting chronic inflammation. This double-edged effect helps explain why stressed individuals often experience both increased susceptibility to colds and higher rates of inflammatory conditions.

Metabolic systems demonstrate clear signatures of allostatic load through changes in glucose regulation, lipid metabolism, and body fat distribution. The repeated mobilization of energy resources during stress can lead to insulin resistance, metabolic syndrome, and increased abdominal fat - all risk factors for type 2 diabetes and cardiovascular disease.

The brain proves particularly sensitive to accumulating allostatic load. Chronic stress exposure can alter neural circuits, affecting memory, emotion regulation, and decision-making abilities. The hippocampus, crucial for memory formation and stress regulation, may actually shrink under prolonged stress exposure, while the amygdala, involved in fear and anxiety, can become hyperactive.

Sleep disturbances both contribute to and result from increasing allostatic load. Poor sleep quality disrupts the body's natural recovery processes, while elevated stress hormones make achieving restful sleep more difficult. This vicious cycle accelerates the accumulation of biological wear and tear.

Hormonal systems show distinct patterns of dysregulation as allostatic load increases. The careful balance of cortisol, adrenaline, and other stress hormones becomes disrupted, leading to abnormal daily rhythms and inappropriate responses to challenges. These hormonal changes can affect everything from mood to immune function to reproductive health.

The digestive system reflects accumulating allostatic load through changes in gut function and microbiome composition. Chronic stress can alter intestinal permeability, disrupt beneficial bacterial communities, and impair nutrient absorption. These changes not only affect digestion but can influence immune function and even mental health through the gut-brain axis.

Cellular aging accelerates under high allostatic load, as evidenced by shortened telomeres - the protective caps on our chromosomes. This cellular wear and tear can lead to premature aging at both the cellular and organismal levels, potentially reducing both healthspan and lifespan.

Social and environmental factors significantly influence the rate at which allostatic load accumulates. Poverty, discrimination, and lack of social support can all accelerate the buildup of biological wear and tear. Conversely, strong social connections, economic security, and access to natural environments can help buffer against accumulating allostatic load.

Individual differences in genetics and early life experiences affect susceptibility to allostatic load. Some people show greater biological resilience to stress, while others accumulate damage more quickly. Understanding these differences helps explain why similar stressors can have varying impacts on different individuals.

The good news is that allostatic load isn't simply a one-way street toward decline. Through targeted interventions and lifestyle changes, we can reduce its accumulation and even reverse some of its effects. Regular physical activity, stress management practices, adequate sleep, and proper nutrition all play crucial roles in maintaining healthy adaptation capacity.

The timing of interventions proves crucial in managing allostatic load. Early intervention, before significant damage accumulates, offers the best opportunity for maintaining health. However, benefits can be achieved at any stage through appropriate lifestyle modifications and stress management strategies.

Understanding allostatic load highlights the importance of creating environments and lifestyles that support healthy adaptation while minimizing unnecessary stress exposure. This understanding can guide both individual health practices and broader social policies aimed at promoting population health and reducing health disparities.

Chapter 2: The Foundations of Allostatic Architecture

Mapping the Bodys Regulatory Systems

The human body operates through an intricate network of regulatory systems that work in concert to maintain life and respond to changing conditions. These interconnected systems form a sophisticated map of biological control, each playing crucial roles while maintaining constant communication with one another.

At the heart of this regulatory network lies the nervous system, split into central and peripheral components. The brain and spinal cord form the central command center, processing information and coordinating responses. The peripheral nervous system extends throughout the body, divided into voluntary and autonomic branches. The autonomic nervous system further splits into sympathetic ("fight or flight") and parasympathetic ("rest and digest") divisions, providing moment-to-moment control of vital functions.

The endocrine system serves as a chemical messaging network, releasing hormones that travel through the bloodstream to influence target tissues. The hypothalamus and pituitary gland form the master control center, regulating hormone production from various glands including the thyroid, adrenals, and gonads. These hormones influence everything from metabolism and growth to reproduction and stress responses.

Immune regulation involves a complex network of cells, tissues, and molecules that protect against threats while maintaining tissue health. This system must carefully balance aggressive responses against harmful invaders with tolerance of beneficial organisms and the body's own tissues. The immune system maintains continuous dialogue with the nervous and endocrine systems, creating a psychoneuroimmune network that influences both physical and mental health.

The cardiovascular system provides essential regulatory functions through blood flow control. Complex mechanisms adjust heart rate, blood pressure, and vessel tone to ensure adequate oxygen and nutrient delivery to tissues. Local and systemic regulatory mechanisms work together to direct blood flow where needed, while maintaining overall cardiovascular stability.

Metabolic regulation orchestrates the complex processes of energy production, storage, and utilization. The liver serves as a central metabolic hub, coordinating with muscle, fat tissue, and other organs to maintain stable blood sugar levels and energy availability. This system responds to both immediate energy demands and longer-term nutritional status.

Temperature regulation exemplifies the integration of multiple systems working together. The hypothalamus monitors body temperature, while the autonomic nervous system adjusts blood flow, sweating, and metabolic rate to maintain optimal temperature. This thermoregulatory system must balance heat production with heat loss across varying environmental conditions.

The respiratory system regulates gas exchange through sophisticated control of breathing rate and depth. Chemoreceptors monitor blood oxygen and carbon dioxide levels, while mechanoreceptors track lung inflation. This information integrates in the brainstem to adjust breathing patterns, ensuring optimal gas exchange under varying conditions.

Fluid and electrolyte balance involves complex interaction between the kidneys, endocrine system, and cardiovascular system. The kidneys filter blood and adjust water and mineral excretion, while hormones like vasopressin and aldosterone fine-tune these processes. This system maintains crucial stability in the body's internal environment.

The digestive system regulates nutrient processing through coordinated mechanical and chemical activities. Local nervous system control combines with hormonal signals to adjust digestive processes based on meal timing and composition. The gut microbiome adds another regulatory layer, influencing both local and systemic function.

Circadian regulation coordinates various physiological processes with environmental light-dark cycles. The suprachiasmatic nucleus in the brain serves as a master clock, synchronizing numerous peripheral clocks throughout the body. This temporal organization optimizes biological functions across the 24-hour day.

The reproductive system demonstrates complex regulation through hormonal feedback loops that control fertility cycles and reproductive function. This system integrates with other regulatory systems, responding to energy availability, stress levels, and environmental conditions.

Bone and calcium regulation involves multiple systems working together to maintain both structural integrity and crucial mineral balance. The parathyroid glands, kidneys, and bone tissue coordinate through various hormones to maintain stable calcium levels while supporting bone health.

Growth and development regulation extends across the lifespan, involving complex interaction between hormones, cellular signals, and environmental factors. This system must balance tissue maintenance and repair with available resources while responding to changing demands.

Pain regulation involves sophisticated neural networks that process and modulate pain signals. This system must balance protective pain responses with the need to function, involving complex interaction between sensory, emotional, and cognitive processes.

Understanding these regulatory systems reveals their remarkable integration and adaptability. Each system maintains some degree of local control while remaining responsive to central coordination. This hierarchical organization allows for both rapid local responses and coordinated whole-body adaptation to changing conditions.

The mapping of these regulatory systems continues to reveal new connections and control mechanisms. This understanding proves crucial for maintaining health and developing therapeutic approaches when regulation falters. Recognition of these systems' interconnected nature highlights the importance of holistic approaches to health maintenance and disease treatment.

Neural Networks and Health

Neural networks within the human body form an intricate web of connections that profoundly influence health and well-being through complex patterns of communication and regulation. These networks extend far beyond the brain, creating sophisticated systems that control everything from basic bodily functions to complex emotional responses.

The brain's neural networks serve as central processors, constantly receiving, interpreting, and responding to information from throughout the body. These networks organize themselves into specialized regions while maintaining remarkable flexibility. Through neuroplasticity, they can reorganize and adapt based on experience, learning, and environmental demands.

Stress response networks illustrate the sophisticated interaction between neural circuits and health outcomes. When facing a challenge, networks in the amygdala, hypothalamus, and brainstem coordinate to initiate appropriate physiological responses. These same networks can either protect or damage health depending on their patterns of activation and the availability of recovery periods.

The gut-brain axis demonstrates how neural networks extend beyond the central nervous system. The enteric nervous system, often called the "second brain," contains millions of neurons that regulate digestion and communicate bidirectionally with the brain. This neural highway influences not only digestive health but also mood, behavior, and immune function.

Pain processing networks reveal the complexity of neural influence on health experiences. These networks involve not just sensory processing but also emotional and cognitive components. Understanding these networks helps explain why pain experiences vary significantly between individuals and how emotional states can modulate pain perception.

Immune system function depends heavily on neural network regulation. Neurons communicate directly with immune cells, influencing their behavior and activity. This neuroimmune communication affects inflammation levels, wound healing, and resistance to disease. Disruption of these networks can lead to both immune suppression and excessive inflammation.

Sleep regulation relies on intricate neural networks that balance wake-promoting and sleep-inducing circuits. These networks coordinate with circadian rhythms to maintain healthy sleep-wake cycles. Disruption of these networks affects not just sleep quality but overall health, including metabolic function, immune response, and cognitive performance.

Memory networks demonstrate how neural connections influence both cognitive function and physical health. These networks not only store information but also guide behavioral responses and emotional regulation. Strong memory networks support better health decisions and more effective stress management strategies.

The autonomic nervous system networks control crucial involuntary functions through sympathetic and parasympathetic branches. These networks must maintain careful balance to support healthy organ function. Dysfunction in these networks can lead to various health problems, from digestive issues to cardiovascular disease.

Emotion regulation networks play a vital role in both mental and physical health. These networks process emotional information and coordinate appropriate responses. Their function influences stress resilience, social relationships, and various health behaviors that impact overall well-being.

Motor control networks extend throughout the body, coordinating movement and maintaining posture. These networks adapt through practice and experience, supporting physical activity and exercise - crucial components of health maintenance. They also influence pain experiences and movement efficiency.

Reward networks influence health-related behaviors through their role in motivation and pleasure. These networks affect everything from food choices to exercise habits to social interactions. Understanding their function helps explain both healthy and unhealthy behavioral patterns.

The hypothalamic networks serve as crucial regulators of multiple body systems. These networks control hormone release, appetite, temperature, and various other physiological functions. Their proper function is essential for maintaining healthy internal balance.

Social behavior networks demonstrate how neural systems influence health through interpersonal connections. These networks process social information and guide interactions with others. Strong social networks, supported by healthy neural function, contribute significantly to overall health outcomes.

Learning networks show remarkable adaptability, allowing for the acquisition of new health-promoting behaviors and coping strategies. These networks can be strengthened through practice, supporting better health choices and more effective stress management.

Sensory processing networks filter and interpret information from the environment, influencing how we respond to potential threats and opportunities. Their function affects stress responses, social interactions, and various health-related behaviors.

The prefrontal networks play crucial roles in decision-making and impulse control, directly affecting health choices and behaviors. These networks help balance immediate desires against long-term health goals, supporting better lifestyle choices.

Understanding neural networks' influence on health highlights the importance of supporting their healthy function through appropriate lifestyle choices. Regular physical activity, adequate sleep, stress management, and social connection all contribute to maintaining robust neural networks.

Recovery and restoration of neural networks requires attention to both physical and psychological factors. Proper nutrition, sleep, and stress management support network maintenance and repair. Social support and positive relationships provide crucial input for healthy network function.

The remarkable plasticity of neural networks offers hope for improving health outcomes through targeted interventions. Whether addressing chronic pain, stress-related disorders, or behavioral health challenges, supporting healthy neural network function provides a foundation for better health outcomes.

The Immune Neuro Endocrine Connection

Three major physiological systems - immune, nervous, and endocrine - form an intricate communication network that orchestrates our body's responses to both internal and external challenges. This sophisticated interaction shapes our health, behavior, and ability to adapt to environmental demands.

The immune system's cellular components continuously patrol our body, identifying and responding to potential threats. Yet these immune cells don't work in isolation - they carry receptors for various neurotransmitters and hormones, allowing direct communication with the nervous and endocrine systems. This molecular conversation enables rapid, coordinated responses to challenges while maintaining internal balance.

Stress represents a clear example of this three-way interaction. When we encounter a stressor, the nervous system immediately activates, triggering the release of adrenaline and other neurotransmitters. These signals prompt the endocrine system to release cortisol and other stress hormones, which in turn modify immune function. This cascade can either enhance or suppress immune responses, depending on the nature and duration of the stress.

The hypothalamus serves as a crucial hub in this network, integrating signals from all three systems. This small brain region responds to immune signals, called cytokines, by adjusting hormone production and nervous system activity. When infection strikes, for instance, cytokines trigger the hypothalamus to initiate fever, alter metabolism, and modify behavior - all coordinated responses that help fight the infection.

Circadian rhythms demonstrate another aspect of this tripartite relationship. The brain's master clock coordinates daily patterns of hormone release, which in turn influence immune cell activity. Immune cells show daily variations in their function, with certain aspects of immunity peaking at specific times. Understanding these patterns helps explain why disrupted sleep and irregular schedules can compromise immune function.

The gut provides a fascinating example of immune-neuro-endocrine interaction. The digestive system contains its own nervous system, hosts a large proportion of our immune cells, and produces various hormones. This local network communicates continuously with the brain, influencing mood, behavior, and overall health. The gut microbiome adds another layer of complexity, producing compounds that affect all three systems.

Chronic inflammation illustrates how disruption of this network can lead to health problems. Inflammatory signals from the immune system can alter both hormone production and neural function. These changes can create self-reinforcing cycles of inflammation, hormonal imbalance, and nervous system dysfunction, contributing to various chronic diseases.

Early life experiences profoundly shape the development of this three-way communication network. Stress, nutrition, and environmental factors during development can permanently alter how these systems interact. These early influences help explain why childhood experiences can have lasting effects on health and disease susceptibility.

Exercise provides a powerful example of how beneficial stress can strengthen this network. Physical activity temporarily activates stress responses but, when followed by recovery, leads to improved communication between all three systems. Regular exercise enhances immune function, optimizes hormone levels, and supports healthy neural signaling.

The aging process affects all three systems and their communication networks. Immune function typically declines, hormone levels change, and neural signaling may become less efficient. However, maintaining healthy lifestyle habits can help preserve the integrity of this network, supporting better health outcomes with age.

Social relationships significantly influence this tripartite system. Positive social connections can enhance immune function, optimize hormone levels, and support healthy neural signaling. Conversely, social isolation or conflict can disrupt this network, potentially contributing to various health problems.

Emotional states demonstrate the bidirectional nature of these interactions. While hormones and immune signals can influence mood and behavior, emotional experiences also affect immune function and hormone levels. This explains how psychological interventions can have physical health benefits and vice versa.

Sleep serves as a crucial period for maintaining and repairing this communication network. During sleep, immune cells undergo important maintenance processes, hormone levels adjust, and neural circuits are optimized. Poor sleep can disrupt this essential maintenance, potentially compromising health.

Nutrition plays a vital role in supporting healthy immune-neuro-endocrine communication. Various nutrients serve as building blocks for neurotransmitters, hormones, and immune cells. Additionally, dietary patterns can influence inflammation levels, hormone production, and neural signaling.

Environmental toxins can disrupt this delicate network by interfering with hormone signaling, triggering inflammation, or affecting neural function. Understanding these influences helps explain why reducing exposure to environmental toxins supports better health outcomes.

The therapeutic implications of understanding this three-way communication network are profound. Interventions targeting any one system can influence the others, offering multiple approaches to supporting health. This understanding supports integrative treatment approaches that consider all three systems together.

Recovery from illness or injury requires coordinated responses from all three systems. Supporting healthy immune-neuro-endocrine communication can enhance healing and recovery processes. This highlights the importance of addressing physical, emotional, and environmental factors in health restoration.

Chapter 3: Building Resilience Through Allostatic Design

Stress Management Strategies

Effective stress management begins with understanding that stress itself isn't inherently harmful - it's our response to stressors and our ability to recover that determines its impact on our health. Modern life presents numerous challenges that can trigger our stress response, making it crucial to develop robust coping strategies.

Physical exercise stands as one of the most powerful stress management tools available. When we engage in regular physical activity, our bodies release endorphins, reduce stress hormones, and improve our resilience to future stressors. Even brief periods of movement, such as a ten-minute walk, can provide immediate stress relief while contributing to long-term stress resistance.

Breathing techniques offer readily accessible stress management tools that can be employed anywhere, anytime. Deep diaphragmatic breathing activates the parasympathetic nervous system, promoting relaxation and reducing anxiety. The 4-7-8 breathing pattern, where you inhale for four counts, hold for seven, and exhale for eight, proves particularly effective in calming the nervous system.

Mindfulness meditation practices help break the cycle of stress by bringing attention to the present moment. Regular meditation practice strengthens our ability to observe thoughts and emotions without becoming overwhelmed by them. Starting with just five minutes daily can build a foundation for more extended practice as comfort and skill develop.

Sleep hygiene plays a crucial role in stress management. Establishing consistent sleep patterns, creating a relaxing bedtime routine, and maintaining a cool, dark sleeping environment help ensure restorative rest. Quality sleep enhances emotional regulation and builds resilience against daily stressors.

Social connections provide vital support during stressful periods. Maintaining strong relationships and seeking support from friends, family, or professional counselors helps process difficult emotions and gain new perspectives on challenging situations. Regular social interaction, even virtually, can buffer against stress's negative effects.

Time management strategies help prevent stress from overwhelming daily life. Breaking large tasks into smaller, manageable steps, setting realistic priorities, and learning to say no to non-essential commitments can significantly reduce stress levels. Creating daily schedules that include breaks and recovery periods proves essential.

Nutrition significantly influences our stress response. A balanced diet rich in whole foods provides the nutrients necessary for optimal stress hormone regulation. Limiting caffeine, alcohol, and processed foods while increasing intake of vegetables, fruits, and omega-3 fatty acids supports better stress management.

Nature exposure offers powerful stress-reducing benefits. Spending time outdoors, whether in urban parks or wilderness areas, lowers cortisol levels and promotes relaxation. Even brief nature encounters, such as tending to houseplants or watching nature videos, can provide stress relief.

Creative expression provides an effective outlet for processing stress and emotions. Activities like journaling, art-making, music, or dance offer healthy ways to release tension and gain perspective on stressful situations. These practices need not produce masterpieces to be beneficial - the process itself provides value.

Cognitive reframing techniques help manage stress by changing how we interpret challenging situations. Learning to identify and challenge negative thought patterns, developing more balanced perspectives, and practicing self-compassion can significantly reduce stress's emotional impact.

Body-based practices like progressive muscle relaxation, yoga, or tai chi help release physical tension while promoting mental calm. These activities improve body awareness, making it easier to recognize and address stress responses before they become overwhelming.

Establishing boundaries proves essential for long-term stress management. Learning to set limits with work, technology use, and personal relationships helps prevent chronic stress from developing. Clear boundaries create space for recovery and self-care.

Regular relaxation practices, such as warm baths, massage, or listening to calming music, activate the relaxation response and counter stress's effects. Incorporating these activities into daily routines provides reliable stress relief and promotes overall well-being.

Time in solitude allows for processing emotions and recharging energy reserves. Creating periods of quiet reflection, away from external demands and digital distractions, helps maintain emotional balance and stress resilience.

Professional support through counseling or therapy can provide valuable tools for managing chronic stress. These relationships offer safe spaces to explore stressors, develop coping strategies, and address underlying issues contributing to stress.

Hobby engagement offers healthy distraction from stressors while providing opportunities for flow states and enjoyment. Regular participation in enjoyable activities that challenge and engage us helps maintain perspective during stressful periods.

Environmental organization reduces daily stress by creating calm, orderly spaces. Regular decluttering, maintaining organized systems, and creating peaceful environments at home and work minimize unnecessary stress triggers.

Stress monitoring through journaling or tracking apps helps identify patterns and triggers. This awareness enables proactive stress management and more effective intervention before stress becomes overwhelming.

The key to successful stress management lies in developing a personalized combination of these strategies, regularly practicing them, and adjusting approaches as needs change. Building these skills takes time and patience, but the investment yields significant returns in improved health and well-being.

Sleep Architecture and Recovery

Sleep unfolds as a precisely orchestrated symphony of neural activity, cycling through distinct stages that each serve vital roles in physical and mental recovery. Understanding these intricate patterns helps reveal why quality sleep proves fundamental to health and performance.

The architecture of sleep consists of four non-REM stages and REM sleep, each characterized by unique brain wave patterns, muscle activity, and physiological processes. As we drift into slumber, our brain waves slow and become more synchronized, marking the transition through increasingly deeper states of rest.

Light sleep, comprising stages one and two, serves as a bridge between wakefulness and deeper sleep states. During these initial stages, heart rate gradually slows, body temperature drops, and muscle activity diminishes. Brief bursts of brain activity called sleep spindles appear, playing crucial roles in memory consolidation and learning.

Deep sleep, also known as slow-wave sleep, represents the most restorative phase of non-REM sleep. During this stage, the brain produces powerful delta waves while the body undergoes intensive physical repair. Growth hormone secretion peaks, supporting tissue repair, muscle growth, and immune system function. This stage proves particularly important for athletic recovery and physical rehabilitation.

REM sleep, characterized by rapid eye movements and vivid dreams, typically occurs every 90 minutes throughout the night. During REM sleep, the brain becomes highly active while the body enters a state of temporary paralysis. This stage plays vital roles in emotional processing, creativity, and memory consolidation, helping integrate new experiences with existing knowledge.

Sleep cycles repeat throughout the night, but their composition changes. Earlier cycles contain more deep sleep, while later cycles feature more REM sleep. This pattern optimizes both physical and mental recovery, highlighting the importance of getting sufficient total sleep time to benefit from all stages.

Recovery during sleep extends far beyond simple rest. The glymphatic system, the brain's waste clearance mechanism, becomes highly active during sleep, removing metabolic byproducts and potentially harmful proteins. This cleansing process helps explain why sleep deprivation can significantly impair cognitive function and emotional regulation.

Muscle recovery accelerates during sleep through increased protein synthesis and decreased protein breakdown. Athletes and individuals engaging in physical training particularly benefit from this nocturnal repair process. Growth hormone secretion during deep sleep promotes tissue healing and adaptation to training stimuli.

Memory consolidation occurs throughout different sleep stages, with each type of sleep contributing uniquely to learning and skill development. While deep sleep strengthens factual memories, REM sleep enhances procedural memory and creative problem-solving abilities. This complementary process optimizes both knowledge retention and skill acquisition.

Emotional recovery relies heavily on healthy sleep architecture. During REM sleep, the brain processes emotional experiences while temporarily reducing stress hormone levels. This combination helps regulate emotional responses and build resilience to future stressors. Poor sleep often manifests first in emotional volatility and decreased stress tolerance.

The immune system undergoes significant enhancement during sleep, with different sleep stages supporting various aspects of immune function. The production and distribution of immune cells increase, while inflammatory markers typically decrease. This balance helps explain why adequate sleep proves crucial for fighting infections and maintaining overall health.

Hormonal regulation depends heavily on proper sleep architecture. The release of growth hormone, testosterone, and other anabolic hormones peaks during deep sleep, while cortisol levels naturally decrease. This hormonal environment promotes recovery and adaptation while reducing stress-related damage.

Recovery from injury accelerates during sleep through enhanced tissue repair processes and reduced inflammation. The body prioritizes healing during sleep, directing energy and resources toward damaged tissues. This explains why sleep disruption can significantly delay recovery from injuries or surgical procedures.

Cognitive recovery occurs throughout all sleep stages but particularly benefits from uninterrupted sleep cycles. The brain consolidates learning, clears waste products, and optimizes neural networks during sleep. This process supports better focus, decision-making, and creative thinking during waking hours.

Environmental factors significantly influence sleep architecture. Temperature, light exposure, noise levels, and bedding comfort can all affect the progression through sleep stages. Optimizing these factors helps ensure more restorative sleep and better recovery outcomes.

Age-related changes in sleep architecture require adaptation of sleep strategies. While deep sleep typically decreases with age, its importance for recovery remains crucial. Adjusting sleep timing, environment, and pre-sleep routines can help maintain sleep quality despite these natural changes.

Recovery from jet lag or shift work requires particular attention to sleep architecture. These disruptions can fragment sleep stages and impair the normal cycling through sleep states. Strategic light exposure, timing of meals, and sleep scheduling can help realign sleep architecture with new time zones or schedules.

The relationship between exercise and sleep architecture demonstrates important considerations for training and recovery. While exercise generally improves sleep quality, intense training too close to bedtime can disrupt sleep architecture. Understanding this relationship helps optimize both training timing and recovery potential.

Monitoring sleep quality through attention to morning freshness, daytime energy levels, and recovery markers provides valuable feedback about sleep architecture. While consumer sleep tracking devices offer interesting insights, subjective feelings of restoration often provide the most practical guidance for sleep optimization.

Movement and Physical Adaptation

Physical adaptation through movement represents one of the most fundamental aspects of human development and ongoing health. Our bodies constantly respond and adapt to the movement demands we place upon them, following a remarkable process of breakdown and rebuilding that ultimately leads to greater strength, endurance, and resilience.

The principle of progressive overload stands at the heart of physical adaptation. When we challenge our bodies with movement that exceeds our current capabilities – but remains within our adaptive capacity – our systems respond by becoming stronger and more efficient. This process occurs across multiple time scales, from immediate responses to long-term structural changes.

Muscular adaptation begins at the cellular level, where movement triggers the production of proteins that strengthen muscle fibers and improve their contractile abilities. Regular movement challenges lead to increased muscle fiber size, enhanced neural recruitment patterns, and improved energy utilization within the muscle tissue. These adaptations result in greater strength, power, and endurance capacity.

Skeletal adaptation follows Wolff's Law, where bone tissue remodels in response to the forces placed upon it. Weight-bearing movements stimulate bone density increases, while a lack of such stimulus leads to bone loss. This principle proves particularly important during development and aging, where appropriate movement can significantly influence bone health.

Cardiovascular adaptation occurs through regular movement challenges that stress the heart and blood vessels. The heart muscle becomes stronger and more efficient, blood volume increases, and new capillaries develop to better serve working muscles. These changes improve oxygen delivery throughout the body and enhance overall endurance capacity.

Neurological adaptation manifests through improved movement patterns and coordination. Regular practice of specific movements enhances the brain's ability to recruit appropriate muscle fibers and coordinate complex actions. This neural plasticity allows for the development of new skills and the refinement of existing movement patterns.

Connective tissue responds to movement by becoming stronger and more resilient. Tendons, ligaments, and fascia adapt to movement demands by altering their structure and composition. Regular, appropriate loading helps maintain the health and elasticity of these tissues, while excessive stress or insufficient recovery can lead to injury.

Energy systems adapt specifically to the type of movement demands placed upon them. Short, intense efforts improve anaerobic capacity, while longer-duration activities enhance aerobic efficiency. The body becomes more skilled at utilizing different energy sources and managing waste products based on the movement patterns it regularly encounters.

Recovery capacity improves through consistent movement practice. The body becomes more efficient at repairing tissue damage, clearing metabolic waste products, and restoring energy reserves. This enhanced recovery ability allows for more frequent or intense movement sessions while reducing the risk of overtraining.

Hormonal responses to movement contribute significantly to adaptation. Exercise triggers the release of growth hormone, testosterone, and other anabolic hormones that promote tissue repair and adaptation. Regular movement helps optimize hormonal profiles for better health and performance.

Movement variability plays a crucial role in developing robust adaptation. Exposing the body to different movement patterns, loads, and intensities creates more comprehensive adaptation and reduces the risk of overuse injuries. This variety also helps maintain movement interest and motivation.

Environmental adaptation occurs through movement in different conditions. Training in heat, cold, or altitude stimulates specific physiological responses that enhance performance and survival capabilities. These environmental challenges add another dimension to physical adaptation.

Age-related considerations influence how we adapt to movement. While the basic principles remain constant, the rate and extent of adaptation change throughout life. Understanding these differences helps optimize movement selection and progression for different age groups.

Injury recovery represents a specific form of adaptation, where movement helps guide the healing process. Appropriate movement during rehabilitation stimulates tissue repair while preventing compensatory patterns that could lead to future problems.

Sleep quality significantly influences physical adaptation. During sleep, the body repairs tissue damage, consolidates movement patterns, and optimizes hormonal responses. Poor sleep can significantly impair adaptation and increase injury risk.

Nutrition supports movement adaptation through providing necessary building blocks for tissue repair and energy production. Proper nutrient timing and selection can enhance recovery and adaptation from movement challenges.

Mental adaptation accompanies physical changes, as regular movement builds confidence, reduces anxiety, and improves stress management capabilities. This psychological adaptation often transfers to other areas of life, enhancing overall resilience.

Movement skill acquisition follows predictable patterns but varies among individuals. Understanding these patterns helps create appropriate progression in movement complexity and intensity, optimizing adaptation while minimizing injury risk.

Long-term adaptation requires careful balance between challenge and recovery. While consistent movement proves essential for ongoing adaptation, adequate rest periods allow for proper tissue repair and prevent overtraining syndrome.

The social aspects of movement can enhance adaptation through motivation, accountability, and shared experience. Group activities often lead to greater adherence and more consistent progression in movement capacity.

Monitoring adaptation through objective and subjective measures helps optimize movement selection and progression. Regular assessment of strength, endurance, mobility, and recovery status guides program adjustments for continued adaptation.

Nutritional Support for Resilience

Nutritional resilience forms the cornerstone of our body's ability to adapt, recover, and thrive under various stressors. The foods we consume provide not just calories, but essential information that guides our cellular function, hormone production, and immune response.

Protein intake plays a crucial role in building resilience, providing the building blocks necessary for tissue repair and immune system function. High-quality protein sources such as fish, eggs, lean meats, and plant-based alternatives supply essential amino acids that support muscle maintenance and recovery from physical stress. The timing of protein consumption throughout the day helps optimize its utilization for repair and adaptation.

Healthy fats serve as both structural components and signaling molecules in our bodies. Omega-3 fatty acids, found abundantly in fatty fish, flaxseeds, and walnuts, help regulate inflammation and support brain health. Medium-chain triglycerides provide readily available energy sources that can enhance cognitive function during periods of stress.

Complex carbohydrates stabilize blood sugar levels, providing sustained energy that supports both physical and mental resilience. Whole grains, legumes, and starchy vegetables offer not just energy, but also fiber and micronutrients that support gut health and immune function. The gut-brain axis significantly influences our stress response and emotional resilience.

Micronutrients play essential roles in energy production, immune function, and stress adaptation. Magnesium, often depleted during stress, supports muscle recovery and sleep quality. Zinc strengthens immune response and wound healing. B-vitamins facilitate energy production and neurotransmitter synthesis, crucial for mental resilience.

Antioxidant-rich foods protect our cells from stress-induced damage. Colorful fruits and vegetables provide polyphenols, flavonoids, and other compounds that combat oxidative stress. Berries, leafy greens, and bright-colored vegetables offer particularly potent protection against cellular damage.

Hydration status significantly impacts our resilience to physical and mental challenges. Beyond water, electrolyte balance supports proper nerve function and cellular communication. Natural sources of electrolytes include coconut water, mineral-rich vegetables, and sea salt.

Adaptogenic herbs and spices enhance our body's ability to handle stress. Turmeric, ginger, and holy basil possess anti-inflammatory properties while supporting immune function. These traditional ingredients have demonstrated benefits for both physical and mental resilience.

Meal timing influences our circadian rhythm and stress response. Regular eating patterns help stabilize blood sugar and cortisol levels, supporting better stress adaptation. Strategic meal timing around physical activity optimizes recovery and adaptation.

Gut health fundamentally affects our resilience through immune function and neurotransmitter production. Fermented foods provide beneficial bacteria that support digestive health and immune response. Fiber-rich foods feed these beneficial bacteria, creating a robust microbiome.

Pre-exercise nutrition supports performance and reduces stress impact. Light, easily digestible meals containing both carbohydrates and protein optimize energy availability while minimizing digestive stress. Post-exercise nutrition accelerates recovery and adaptation.

Recovery nutrition focuses on replenishing energy stores and providing materials for repair. The post-exercise window offers an opportunity to enhance adaptation through strategic nutrient timing. This period proves particularly important for athletes and physically active individuals.

Sleep-supporting nutrients include tryptophan-rich foods, magnesium, and herbs like chamomile. These compounds help regulate sleep-wake cycles and enhance sleep quality, crucial for stress recovery and resilience building.

Anti-inflammatory foods help manage the physical impact of stress. Omega-3 fatty acids, curcumin, and certain fruits and vegetables help modulate inflammation levels, supporting faster recovery from physical and mental challenges.

Cognitive function receives support from specific nutrients including omega-3 fatty acids, flavonoids, and choline. These compounds enhance brain plasticity and protect against stress-induced cognitive decline. Regular consumption of these nutrients supports mental resilience.

Energy production depends on adequate micronutrient status. Iron, B-vitamins, and CoQ10 play crucial roles in cellular energy generation. Deficiencies in these nutrients can significantly impact our resilience to physical and mental challenges.

Immune system support requires a broad spectrum of nutrients. Vitamin C, vitamin D, zinc, and selenium play particularly important roles in maintaining robust immune function. Regular consumption of nutrient-dense foods helps maintain strong immune defenses.

Hormone balance receives significant influence from our nutritional choices. Healthy fats support steroid hormone production, while protein provides building blocks for various hormones and neurotransmitters. This hormonal balance significantly affects our stress resilience.

Environmental toxin exposure can be mitigated through strategic nutrition. Cruciferous vegetables enhance detoxification pathways, while antioxidant-rich foods protect against environmental stressors. Clean, whole food sources minimize exposure to harmful compounds.

Long-term nutritional strategies prove more effective than short-term interventions. Building resilience through nutrition requires consistent, sustainable practices rather than extreme approaches. Small, consistent improvements in food choices accumulate to create significant benefits over time.

Environmental Optimization

Environmental factors profoundly influence our physical and mental performance, shaping our ability to recover, adapt, and thrive. The spaces we inhabit, from our bedrooms to our workplaces, create a complex web of stimuli that directly impact our biological systems and behavioral patterns.

Light exposure serves as a primary environmental factor affecting our circadian rhythm and hormonal balance. Natural daylight, particularly morning sunlight, helps regulate our sleep-wake cycle by suppressing melatonin and boosting cortisol at appropriate times. Strategic light management, including reducing blue light exposure in the evening and maintaining bright environments during active hours, supports optimal physiological functioning.

Temperature regulation plays a crucial role in both performance and recovery. The human body operates most efficiently within a narrow temperature range, typically between 20-22°C (68-72°F) for active work and slightly cooler for sleep. Heat exposure can enhance cardiovascular adaptation when properly dosed, while cold exposure stimulates metabolic improvements and recovery processes.

Air quality significantly impacts cognitive function and physical performance. Well-ventilated spaces with low levels of carbon dioxide and pollutants support better concentration and energy levels. Indoor plants, proper ventilation systems, and regular air circulation help maintain optimal air quality while reducing the accumulation of harmful compounds.

Sound management affects both productivity and recovery. Background noise at appropriate levels can enhance focus for certain tasks, while complete silence often proves optimal for deep work and sleep. Natural sounds, such as flowing water or forest ambiance, can reduce stress and improve cognitive performance.

Physical space organization influences behavior and mental state. Clutter-free environments reduce cognitive load and stress levels, while well-organized spaces promote efficient movement and task completion. The arrangement of furniture and equipment should support natural movement patterns and minimize unnecessary physical strain.

Color psychology impacts mood and energy levels. Blue and green tones promote calm and focus, while warmer colors can enhance creativity and social interaction. Strategic use of color in different spaces supports various activities and psychological states throughout the day.

Electromagnetic field exposure from modern technology can influence sleep quality and stress levels. Creating low-EMF zones, particularly in sleeping areas, may support better recovery and regulatory processes. Simple practices like keeping electronics away from the bed and using airplane mode during sleep can reduce potential disruptions.

Natural elements incorporated into living and working spaces enhance well-being and cognitive function. Access to views of nature, even through windows, reduces stress and improves attention.

Indoor plants, natural materials, and organic shapes create more restorative environments.

Humidity levels affect respiratory health and comfort. Maintaining optimal humidity between 40-60% supports immune function while preventing the growth of mold and bacteria. Proper humidity also improves skin health and sleep quality.

Ergonomic design in work and rest spaces prevents unnecessary physical stress and supports natural movement patterns. Adjustable furniture, proper monitor heights, and supportive sleeping surfaces minimize physical strain while promoting better posture and movement quality.

Social space design influences interaction patterns and stress levels. Creating areas that support both collaboration and privacy allows for balanced social engagement and personal recovery. The arrangement of common spaces can either promote or hinder healthy social interactions.

Storage solutions affect both physical and mental organization. Easy access to frequently used items reduces physical strain and cognitive load. Thoughtful storage design supports efficient daily routines while minimizing stress and decision fatigue.

Transition zones between different activities help signal behavioral shifts to our nervous system. Creating distinct spaces for work, exercise, and rest supports appropriate energy states and focus levels for each activity. These environmental cues strengthen beneficial habits and routines.

Seasonal adaptations in environmental design maintain comfort and performance throughout the year. Adjusting light exposure, temperature control, and activity spaces according to seasonal changes supports consistent performance despite external variations.

Personal customization within environmental constraints allows for individual optimization while maintaining system-wide benefits. Small adjustments in immediate workspace or recovery areas can significantly impact personal comfort and effectiveness without disrupting shared spaces.

Sustainability considerations in environmental design support long-term well-being. Using eco-friendly materials, maximizing natural light and ventilation, and minimizing resource waste creates healthier spaces while reducing environmental impact.

Technology integration should enhance rather than dominate environmental design. Smart systems for lighting, temperature, and air quality can optimize conditions while remaining unobtrusive. The goal is to support human function rather than create dependency on technological solutions.

Recovery spaces require particular attention to environmental factors. Bedrooms should prioritize sleep quality through darkness, quiet, and temperature control. Relaxation areas benefit from natural elements and minimal technological distraction.

Performance zones need specific environmental considerations based on intended activities. Exercise spaces require good ventilation and appropriate temperature control, while focus work areas benefit from controlled sound levels and optimal lighting.

The cumulative effect of environmental factors creates either supportive or degrading conditions for human performance and recovery. Regular assessment and adjustment of environmental elements ensure continued optimization as needs and circumstances change over time.

Chapter 4: The Mind-Body Interface

Psychological Flexibility

Psychological flexibility represents the cornerstone of mental resilience and emotional well-being. This dynamic capacity allows us to adapt effectively to changing circumstances while maintaining alignment with our core values and long-term objectives. The ability to bend without breaking, to shift perspectives while staying grounded, defines our capacity to thrive in an ever-changing world.

At its heart, psychological flexibility involves accepting our thoughts and emotions without becoming entangled in them. When challenging situations arise, the flexible mind acknowledges discomfort without attempting to suppress or avoid it. This acceptance paradoxically creates space for more effective responses rather than reactive behaviors driven by emotional avoidance.

The development of psychological flexibility begins with present-moment awareness. By cultivating the ability to observe our current experience without judgment, we create a foundation for conscious choice rather than automatic reaction. This mindful stance allows us to recognize when we're caught in rigid thinking patterns or unhelpful behavioral loops.

Values play a crucial role in psychological flexibility. Clear awareness of what matters most to us provides a compass for navigation through difficult circumstances. When we understand our core values, we can make choices that align with these deeper priorities rather than being driven solely by immediate comfort or convenience.

Cognitive defusion techniques help us develop a healthier relationship with our thoughts. By learning to see thoughts as mental events rather than absolute truths, we gain the freedom to choose our responses rather than being controlled by every passing thought. This skill proves particularly valuable when facing self-limiting beliefs or negative thought patterns.

Emotional agility complements cognitive flexibility. The capacity to experience a full range of emotions while maintaining purposeful action enables us to navigate life's challenges more effectively. Rather than being hijacked by strong emotions or attempting to suppress them, we learn to hold them while continuing to move in valued directions.

Behavioral flexibility emerges from this foundation of cognitive and emotional agility. The ability to adjust our actions based on changing circumstances while maintaining sight of our larger goals allows for more effective problem-solving and goal pursuit. This includes knowing when to persist and when to pivot strategies.

Social flexibility involves adapting our interpersonal style while maintaining authentic connection. Different relationships and contexts may require different approaches, but psychological flexibility allows us to adjust without compromising our core values or genuine self-expression.

Recovery from setbacks benefits significantly from psychological flexibility. Rather than becoming stuck in self-criticism or avoidance, flexible thinking allows us to learn from challenges and adjust our approach. This resilience enables faster recovery and more effective adaptation to future challenges.

Time perspective flexibility allows us to shift appropriately between past, present, and future focus. While maintaining present awareness remains important, psychological flexibility includes the ability to learn from past experiences and plan for the future without becoming stuck in either temporal direction.

Decision-making improves through psychological flexibility. By maintaining multiple perspectives and remaining open to new information, we make choices that better serve our long-term interests. This approach helps avoid the pitfalls of rigid thinking or impulsive reactions.

Stress management benefits from psychological flexibility through improved coping strategies. Rather than relying on a single approach, flexible individuals can adapt their stress response based on the specific situation and available resources. This adaptability leads to more effective stress regulation.

Goal pursuit becomes more effective through psychological flexibility. While maintaining commitment to important objectives, flexible individuals can adjust their methods and timelines based on changing circumstances. This balance between persistence and adaptation optimizes goal achievement.

Relationship dynamics improve through psychological flexibility. The ability to see situations from multiple perspectives, adapt communication styles, and maintain boundaries while remaining connected enhances interpersonal effectiveness. This skill proves particularly valuable in managing conflict and building lasting connections.

Professional development benefits from psychological flexibility through enhanced learning and adaptation. The capacity to embrace new challenges, accept feedback, and adjust approaches supports career growth and satisfaction. This flexibility helps navigate organizational changes and professional transitions.

Creative problem-solving expands through psychological flexibility. By remaining open to multiple possibilities and willing to experiment with new approaches, we discover more effective solutions to challenges. This creativity extends beyond traditional problem-solving into innovation and personal growth.

Self-compassion grows alongside psychological flexibility. As we develop the ability to hold difficult experiences with awareness and acceptance, we naturally cultivate a kinder relationship with ourselves. This self-compassion supports continued growth and resilience.

Leadership capabilities enhance through psychological flexibility. The ability to adapt leadership style while maintaining consistent values allows for more effective guidance of others through change and challenge. This flexibility supports both individual and team development.

Life transitions become more manageable through psychological flexibility. Whether facing career changes, relationship shifts, or personal transformations, the ability to adapt while maintaining core stability supports smoother navigation of major life changes.

The practice of psychological flexibility requires ongoing attention and development. Like physical flexibility, it must be maintained through regular exercise and conscious application in daily life. This investment yields significant returns in enhanced resilience and life satisfaction.

Emotional Regulation

Emotional regulation stands as a fundamental skill that shapes our daily experiences, relationships, and long-term well-being. The ability to understand, manage, and respond appropriately to our emotions determines how effectively we navigate life's challenges and opportunities.

Our emotional landscape operates like an intricate ecosystem, where each feeling serves a specific purpose in our survival and growth. Anger alerts us to boundaries being crossed, fear warns us of potential dangers, and joy connects us to what matters most. Understanding these emotional signals allows us to respond more effectively to life's demands.

The foundation of emotional regulation begins with awareness. By developing the capacity to recognize and label our emotional states, we gain the initial tools needed for effective management. This awareness includes noticing physical sensations, thought patterns, and behavioral urges associated with different emotions.

Timing plays a crucial role in emotional regulation. Early recognition of emotional shifts allows for more effective intervention before emotions escalate beyond our control. This early awareness creates space for conscious choice rather than reactive behavior.

Physical regulation serves as an essential component of emotional management. Deep breathing, movement, and other somatic practices help modulate our nervous system's response to emotional stimuli. These physical tools provide immediate access to emotional regulation when cognitive strategies might prove challenging.

The window of tolerance concept helps us understand our optimal zone for emotional processing. Operating within this window allows us to experience emotions without becoming overwhelmed or shut down. Recognizing when we're moving outside this window enables us to take appropriate regulatory action.

Social connection significantly influences our emotional regulation capacity. Secure relationships provide both a safety net for emotional processing and models for effective regulation. The presence of supportive others helps co-regulate our emotional states, particularly during challenging times.

Language shapes our ability to regulate emotions effectively. Developing a rich emotional vocabulary enables more precise identification and expression of our feelings. This precision supports better understanding and more targeted regulation strategies.

Different emotions require different regulation approaches. While some emotions benefit from expression and release, others might need containment or redirection. Learning to match regulation strategies to specific emotional states enhances their effectiveness.

The role of thoughts in emotional regulation cannot be overstated. Our interpretations of events significantly influence our emotional responses. Developing the ability to examine and adjust these interpretations provides a powerful tool for emotional regulation.

Body-based awareness supports sustainable emotional regulation. Recognizing how emotions manifest in our bodies helps us intervene earlier and more effectively. This somatic awareness also provides valuable feedback about the effectiveness of our regulation strategies.

Recovery from emotional intensity requires specific attention. Creating space for emotional processing, whether through solitude, movement, or supportive conversation, allows for natural regulation and integration of emotional experiences.

Boundaries play a crucial role in emotional regulation. Clear personal boundaries help prevent emotional overwhelm while supporting healthy relationships. These boundaries include both internal limits on our emotional exposure and external limits in our interactions with others.

The practice of self-compassion enhances emotional regulation capacity. Treating ourselves with kindness during difficult emotional states reduces secondary stress and supports more effective regulation. This compassionate stance creates space for both acceptance and change.

Environmental factors significantly impact our emotional regulation abilities. Creating supportive environments that match our regulatory needs helps maintain emotional balance. This includes both physical space organization and social environment management.

Routine and structure support consistent emotional regulation. Regular practices that support emotional awareness and management build regulatory capacity over time. These routines become particularly valuable during times of stress or transition.

The relationship between energy management and emotional regulation deserves attention. Adequate rest, nutrition, and physical activity support our regulatory capacity. Depleted physical resources often correlate with diminished emotional regulation abilities.

Professional and personal contexts require different regulatory approaches. Developing context-specific strategies helps navigate various life domains effectively. This flexibility in regulation supports both performance and relationship quality.

Long-term emotional regulation development requires patience and persistence. Like any skill, regulatory capacity builds through consistent practice and application. Small, regular investments in emotional regulation yield significant benefits over time.

Cultural influences shape our emotional regulation strategies and expectations. Understanding these influences helps us develop regulation approaches that honor both personal and cultural contexts. This awareness supports more effective emotional management across different situations.

The integration of emotional regulation with other life skills enhances overall effectiveness. When combined with clear communication, boundary setting, and self-care practices, emotional regulation becomes a powerful tool for personal growth and relationship development.

Cognitive Adaptation

Cognitive adaptation represents our brain's remarkable ability to modify, adjust, and enhance its functioning in response to environmental demands and experiences. This dynamic process shapes our learning, problem-solving abilities, and overall mental performance throughout life.

The brain's plasticity serves as the foundation for cognitive adaptation, allowing neural networks to reorganize and strengthen based on our experiences and practices. This flexibility enables us to acquire new skills, overcome challenges, and maintain mental agility as we age.

Learning strategies play a crucial role in cognitive adaptation. By understanding how our brain processes and stores information, we can develop more effective approaches to skill acquisition and knowledge retention. The spacing effect, for instance, demonstrates how distributed practice sessions lead to better long-term learning compared to cramming.

Memory enhancement occurs through deliberate cognitive adaptation practices. Building strong associative networks, using visualization techniques, and creating meaningful connections between new and existing knowledge strengthens our ability to retain and recall information. These strategies become increasingly important as we face growing information demands.

Problem-solving capabilities expand through exposure to diverse challenges. Each new problem we encounter creates neural pathways that can be applied to future situations. The development of mental models and frameworks allows us to approach novel challenges with greater efficiency and creativity.

Attention management improves through targeted practice. In our increasingly distracting world, the ability to direct and sustain focus becomes crucial. Training our attention through mindfulness practices and structured work periods enhances our cognitive control and processing efficiency.

Pattern recognition skills develop as we expose ourselves to varied experiences and challenges. The brain naturally seeks patterns and relationships, and deliberately engaging with complex problems strengthens this ability. Enhanced pattern recognition supports better decision-making and problem-solving across different domains.

Cognitive flexibility grows through exposure to diverse perspectives and approaches. Engaging with different viewpoints and methods of thinking expands our mental repertoire. This adaptability allows us to navigate complex situations more effectively and find innovative solutions.

Stress resilience builds through understanding and adapting to cognitive demands. Learning to recognize cognitive load and developing strategies to manage it prevents mental fatigue and supports sustained performance. Regular breaks, task prioritization, and environmental optimization all contribute to cognitive resilience.

Language acquisition and development continue throughout life, supporting cognitive adaptation. Exposure to new vocabulary, concepts, and ways of expressing ideas enhances our mental flexibility and communication abilities. Multiple language learning particularly strengthens cognitive control and adaptive capabilities.

Critical thinking skills sharpen through deliberate practice and exposure to challenging ideas. Developing the ability to analyze, evaluate, and synthesize information supports better decision-making and problem-solving. This skill becomes increasingly valuable in our information-rich environment.

Creative thinking expands through cognitive adaptation practices. Engaging in divergent thinking exercises, exploring new perspectives, and combining different ideas in novel ways strengthens our creative capabilities. This creativity supports innovation and adaptive problem-solving.

Social cognition improves through interpersonal interactions and perspective-taking exercises. Understanding others' viewpoints and emotional states enhances our ability to navigate social situations and build stronger relationships. This social adaptability supports both personal and professional success.

Mental models evolve through experience and reflection. Building and refining these internal frameworks allows us to better understand complex systems and make more accurate predictions. Regular updating of these models supports continued cognitive adaptation.

Decision-making processes enhance through exposure to varied situations and outcomes. Learning from both successes and failures helps develop more sophisticated decision strategies. This experiential learning supports better judgment in future situations.

Information processing speed increases through targeted practice and exposure to time-pressured situations. Developing efficient mental shortcuts and recognition patterns allows for faster, more accurate responses to familiar challenges. This processing efficiency supports better performance under pressure.

Metacognition strengthens through deliberate reflection on our thinking processes. Understanding how we learn and solve problems allows us to optimize our cognitive strategies. This self-awareness supports more effective learning and problem-solving approaches.

Error recognition and correction improve through experience and feedback. Developing the ability to quickly identify and adjust mistakes enhances learning and performance. This adaptive capability supports continuous improvement and skill development.

Knowledge integration becomes more sophisticated through cognitive adaptation. The ability to connect information across different domains and apply knowledge in new contexts supports innovative problem-solving and deeper understanding. This integration enhances overall cognitive flexibility.

Long-term cognitive health benefits from continued adaptation and challenge. Engaging in varied mental activities, maintaining social connections, and pursuing new learning opportunities supports cognitive resilience as we age. This ongoing adaptation helps maintain mental sharpness and processing capabilities throughout life.

Regular assessment and adjustment of cognitive strategies ensures continued growth and adaptation. As circumstances and demands change, our approaches to learning and problem-solving must evolve. This dynamic process of cognitive adaptation supports lifelong development and performance enhancement.

Behavioral Modification

Behavioral modification emerges from our understanding that lasting change requires systematic approaches to reshaping our actions and responses. The process begins with recognizing that our behaviors are learned patterns that can be consciously altered through deliberate practice and consistent reinforcement.

Success in changing behavior relies heavily on understanding the triggers and consequences that maintain our current patterns. Every action we take exists within a context of antecedents and outcomes, forming chains of behavior that become increasingly automatic over time. Breaking these chains requires careful observation and strategic intervention at key points.

Environmental design plays a crucial role in supporting behavioral change. By restructuring our surroundings to make desired behaviors easier and unwanted behaviors more difficult, we create natural pathways toward positive change. Something as simple as placing running shoes by the bed can increase morning exercise compliance significantly.

The power of small wins cannot be overstated in behavioral modification. Rather than attempting dramatic transformations overnight, focusing on tiny, manageable changes builds momentum and confidence. These micro-adjustments, when consistently applied, create the foundation for larger behavioral shifts.

Habit stacking represents a powerful strategy for incorporating new behaviors. By attaching desired actions to existing routines, we leverage established neural pathways to build new patterns. For instance, linking a brief meditation practice to your morning coffee ritual increases the likelihood of consistency.

Feedback loops serve as essential tools in behavioral modification. Tracking progress, measuring outcomes, and adjusting approaches based on results creates a dynamic system for continuous improvement. Regular self-monitoring helps maintain motivation and identify areas needing adjustment.

Social support significantly influences behavioral change success. Engaging others in our modification efforts provides accountability, encouragement, and practical assistance. Finding or creating communities with shared goals can dramatically increase the likelihood of sustained change.

Reward systems must be carefully designed to support long-term modification. While immediate rewards can jump-start change, developing intrinsic motivation proves crucial for lasting transformation. Gradually shifting from external rewards to internal satisfaction supports sustainable behavioral change.

Stress management becomes particularly important during behavioral modification efforts. High stress levels can trigger reversion to old patterns, making stress reduction techniques essential components of any change strategy. Building resilience through regular self-care practices supports consistent progress.

Implementation intentions help bridge the gap between goals and actions. Creating specific plans for when, where, and how new behaviors will be executed increases follow-through significantly. These detailed action plans reduce decision fatigue and strengthen commitment.

The role of identity in behavioral modification deserves special attention. Adopting beliefs and self-perceptions aligned with desired behaviors creates powerful internal motivation for change. Viewing ourselves as someone who naturally embodies our target behaviors accelerates transformation.

Recovery strategies prove essential for maintaining progress after setbacks. Understanding that lapses are normal parts of the change process helps prevent temporary slips from becoming complete reversions. Having predetermined plans for getting back on track supports resilience.

Time management skills significantly impact behavioral modification success. Allocating specific times for new behaviors and protecting these time blocks from interruption increases consistency. Strategic scheduling that accounts for energy levels and natural rhythms supports sustainable change.

The power of visualization supports behavioral modification through mental rehearsal. Regularly imagining successful execution of desired behaviors strengthens neural pathways and increases confidence. Detailed mental practice enhances physical performance and behavioral consistency.

Boundary setting plays a crucial role in protecting new behavioral patterns. Learning to communicate limits effectively and maintain them despite external pressure supports lasting change. Clear boundaries prevent environmental factors from derailing modification efforts.

Progressive loading principles apply to behavioral modification just as they do to physical training. Gradually increasing the challenge or complexity of new behaviors builds capability while preventing overwhelm. This measured approach supports sustainable progress and skill development.

Documentation of progress provides valuable motivation and insight. Keeping records of successes, challenges, and adjustments helps identify patterns and optimize strategies. Regular review of these records reinforces commitment and celebrates progress.

Environmental cues require careful management during behavioral modification. Removing triggers for unwanted behaviors while establishing prompts for desired actions creates supportive conditions for change. Strategic placement of visual reminders reinforces new patterns.

Flexibility in approach maintains effectiveness over time. As circumstances change and initial strategies lose impact, being willing to adjust methods while maintaining core goals supports continued progress. Regular evaluation and refinement of techniques prevents stagnation.

The compound effect of consistent behavioral modification creates lasting transformation. Small, daily choices accumulate over time, leading to significant life changes. Understanding this principle helps maintain patience and persistence during the modification process.

Celebration of progress, no matter how small, reinforces positive change. Regular acknowledgment of efforts and achievements builds momentum and maintains motivation. Creating meaningful ways to recognize progress supports long-term commitment to behavioral modification.

Chapter 5: Practical Implementation

Assessment Tools and Biomarkers

Assessment tools and biomarkers serve as essential components in understanding and measuring human performance, health status, and potential interventions. These scientific indicators provide objective data that guide decision-making and track progress across various domains of human optimization.

Blood analysis remains one of the most comprehensive assessment tools available, offering insights into hormonal balance, nutrient levels, inflammatory markers, and metabolic function. Regular blood panels can reveal subtle imbalances before they manifest as noticeable symptoms, allowing for proactive intervention. Key markers like vitamin D, testosterone, cortisol, and inflammatory cytokines provide valuable information about overall health status.

Heart rate variability (HRV) measurements offer a window into autonomic nervous system function and recovery capacity. This powerful biomarker indicates how well the body adapts to stress and recovers from physical and mental demands. Higher HRV generally correlates with better stress resilience and overall health outcomes.

Sleep tracking technology has evolved to provide detailed insights into sleep architecture and quality.

Measuring parameters such as sleep stages, respiratory rate, and movement patterns helps optimize recovery and cognitive performance. These measurements guide interventions to enhance sleep efficiency and overall restoration.

Cognitive assessment tools evaluate various aspects of mental performance, including attention, memory, processing speed, and executive function. Standardized tests and digital platforms can track changes in cognitive capabilities over time, helping identify areas for improvement and measuring the effectiveness of interventions.

Physical performance metrics encompass strength, endurance, flexibility, and power output measurements. These assessments provide objective data about functional capacity and help guide training programs. Regular testing allows for precise tracking of progress and appropriate adjustment of training stimuli.

Genetic testing offers insights into individual predispositions and potential response patterns to various interventions. While genes aren't destiny, understanding genetic variants can help optimize nutrition, exercise, and recovery strategies for individual needs.

Metabolic testing provides detailed information about energy utilization and substrate preference during different activities. Measuring parameters like VO2 max, lactate threshold, and respiratory quotient helps optimize training and nutrition strategies for specific performance goals.

Hormonal panels reveal the complex interplay of endocrine function and its impact on performance and recovery. Regular monitoring of key hormones helps identify imbalances that might affect energy, mood, recovery, and adaptation to training stimuli.

Body composition analysis using advanced techniques like DEXA scans or bioelectrical impedance provides accurate measurements of muscle mass, fat distribution, and bone density. These measurements help track the effectiveness of nutrition and training interventions.

Inflammatory markers serve as crucial indicators of recovery status and overall health. Monitoring these biomarkers helps prevent overtraining and guides appropriate training loads and recovery protocols.

Gut health assessments examine the microbiome composition and digestive function, providing insights into nutrient absorption, immune function, and overall health status. These measurements guide dietary interventions and supplementation strategies.

Neurological assessments evaluate brain function through various methods, including EEG and cognitive testing. These tools help optimize mental performance and track the effectiveness of cognitive enhancement strategies.

Movement analysis using video technology and force plates provides detailed information about biomechanics and movement efficiency. These assessments guide technique improvements and injury prevention strategies.

Psychological assessments measure mental state, stress levels, and emotional well-being. Regular monitoring of these parameters helps maintain optimal psychological function and guides interventions when needed.

Environmental monitoring tools track exposure to various factors that impact performance and health. Measuring air quality, light exposure, and other environmental parameters helps optimize living and training conditions.

Recovery markers include various measurements that indicate restoration status, such as muscle damage markers, inflammatory proteins, and autonomic nervous system function. These indicators help optimize training frequency and intensity.

Nutritional status assessments go beyond basic blood panels to examine micronutrient levels, fatty acid profiles, and amino acid status. These detailed measurements guide precise supplementation and dietary adjustments.

Performance tracking tools integrate various data points to provide comprehensive insights into training effectiveness and adaptation. These systems help identify patterns and optimize training programs for specific outcomes.

Longevity markers examine various aspects of biological aging, including telomere length, DNA methylation patterns, and other age-related biomarkers. These measurements help guide interventions aimed at optimizing healthspan and lifespan.

The integration of multiple assessment tools and biomarkers provides the most comprehensive understanding of human performance and health status. Regular monitoring using various methods allows for precise optimization of interventions and tracking of progress toward specific goals. This systematic approach to measurement and assessment forms the foundation for effective human optimization strategies.

Creating Personal Health Protocols

Personal health protocols form the cornerstone of sustainable wellness and optimal performance. These individualized frameworks serve as daily guides, incorporating various elements of health management into a cohesive system that addresses unique needs, goals, and lifestyle factors.

Developing an effective protocol begins with a thorough assessment of current health status, including physical condition, mental well-being, and environmental influences. This baseline evaluation provides crucial insights for creating targeted interventions that address specific challenges and leverage existing strengths.

Morning routines establish the foundation for daily success. A well-designed morning protocol might include hydration, movement, mindfulness practices, and nutritional timing. The key lies in creating a sequence that energizes both body and mind while remaining practical enough for consistent execution.

Sleep optimization represents a critical component of any health protocol. Establishing consistent sleep and wake times, creating an optimal sleep environment, and developing wind-down routines that signal the body to prepare for rest contribute to better recovery and cognitive function.

Nutritional timing and meal composition require careful consideration within personal protocols. Planning meals around activity levels, work schedules, and individual metabolic patterns helps maintain stable energy levels throughout the day. Strategic nutrient timing supports both performance and recovery goals.

Movement integration throughout the day prevents the negative effects of prolonged sitting. Simple practices like standing meetings, walking breaks, or desk exercises maintain circulation and muscle activation. These micro-movements complement more structured exercise sessions.

Stress management techniques must be woven into daily routines rather than treated as occasional interventions. Regular breathing exercises, meditation sessions, or nature exposure can be scheduled at specific times when stress typically peaks.

Recovery practices deserve equal attention to active pursuits. Incorporating regular massage, mobility work, or other restorative practices prevents burnout and supports sustained performance. Scheduling these activities ensures they receive proper priority.

Environmental optimization plays a crucial role in health protocols. Managing light exposure, air quality, and noise levels creates conditions that support optimal function. Simple adjustments like blue light filtering and proper ventilation can significantly impact well-being.

Social connection must be deliberately incorporated into modern health protocols. Scheduling regular interaction with supportive individuals, whether through shared activities or dedicated social time, supports emotional well-being and stress resilience.

Supplementation strategies require careful timing and selection based on individual needs. Creating systems for consistent supplement intake, including proper storage and tracking, ensures maximum benefit from these interventions.

Regular assessment and adjustment periods must be built into any protocol. Monthly reviews of progress, challenges, and changing needs allow for timely modifications that maintain protocol effectiveness.

Energy management throughout the day requires strategic planning. Matching demanding tasks to peak energy periods while scheduling recovery during natural dips optimizes productivity and reduces stress.

Hydration protocols need specific attention, with scheduled water intake throughout the day. Adding electrolytes or other supplements based on activity levels and environmental conditions supports optimal hydration status.

Technology management deserves dedicated protocol elements. Establishing boundaries around device use, including designated offline periods and screen-free zones, supports better sleep and mental clarity.

Weekend protocols might differ from weekday routines while maintaining core health practices. This flexibility allows for social activities and relaxation while preventing complete deviation from healthy habits.

Travel adaptations of regular protocols ensure consistency during disrupted schedules. Creating modified versions of daily routines that can be executed in various environments maintains health practices during travel.

Seasonal adjustments acknowledge the impact of changing environmental conditions on health needs. Protocols should evolve with variations in daylight, temperature, and activity patterns throughout the year.

Emergency protocols provide clear guidelines for maintaining essential health practices during high-stress periods or unexpected disruptions. Having predetermined modifications helps maintain core habits during challenging times.

Documentation systems support protocol adherence and optimization. Whether using digital tools or paper journals, tracking compliance and outcomes provides valuable data for future adjustments.

Integration with family or household routines ensures sustainability of personal protocols. Finding ways to align individual health practices with family schedules and needs increases long-term success.

Regular review and refinement keeps protocols relevant and effective. Quarterly assessments of protocol elements, combined with outcome measurements, guide evolutionary improvements over time.

The key to successful protocol implementation lies in finding the balance between structure and flexibility. While consistent practices form the foundation of health improvement, rigid adherence can create unnecessary stress. Creating protocols that bend without breaking ensures long-term sustainability and continued progress toward optimal health.

Monitoring and Adjusting Interventions

Successful interventions require vigilant monitoring and strategic adjustments to maintain effectiveness and achieve desired outcomes. The dynamic nature of human physiology and psychology demands an adaptive approach that responds to changing conditions and individual responses.

Regular data collection forms the foundation of effective monitoring. Daily tracking of key metrics, including sleep quality, energy levels, mood, and physical performance, provides crucial feedback about intervention effectiveness. These measurements reveal patterns that might otherwise go unnoticed in the complexity of daily life.

Biomarker testing at scheduled intervals offers objective measures of intervention impact. Blood work, hormone panels, and other clinical measurements provide concrete data about physiological changes. These results guide necessary adjustments to supplementation, nutrition, and other therapeutic approaches.

Subjective feedback plays an equally important role in monitoring interventions. Daily journaling about energy levels, emotional state, and perceived effectiveness helps identify subtle changes that might not appear in objective measurements. This qualitative data often reveals early signs of needed adjustments.

Performance metrics require regular assessment through standardized testing protocols. Whether measuring strength, endurance, cognitive function, or other capabilities, consistent testing methods ensure reliable data for comparison over time. These results help fine-tune training and recovery protocols.

Environmental factors must be considered when evaluating intervention effectiveness. Seasonal changes, work stress, travel, and other external variables can significantly impact results. Accounting for these influences helps distinguish between intervention-related changes and environmental effects.

Adjustment timing requires careful consideration to allow proper evaluation of interventions. While some changes produce immediate effects, others need weeks or months to show meaningful results. Understanding these different time scales prevents premature modifications that might disrupt positive adaptations.

Systematic documentation of adjustments helps track the effectiveness of different approaches. Recording specific changes in protocol, along with subsequent results, builds a valuable database of individual responses. This information guides future modifications and helps identify optimal strategies.

Stress levels significantly influence intervention outcomes and must be monitored closely. Regular assessment of both physical and psychological stress helps predict when adjustments might be necessary. Proactive modifications based on stress levels can prevent decreased effectiveness or negative responses.

Sleep quality serves as a crucial indicator of intervention appropriateness. Changes in sleep patterns often signal the need for protocol adjustments. Monitoring sleep metrics helps maintain the delicate balance between stimulus and recovery.

Energy management throughout the day provides important feedback about intervention effectiveness. Tracking energy patterns helps identify whether current protocols support or hinder daily function. Adjustments can then be made to optimize energy distribution across various activities.

Recovery capacity requires regular assessment to ensure interventions remain beneficial rather than depleting. Monitoring markers of recovery, such as heart rate variability and subjective readiness, helps prevent overreach and maintains productive adaptation.

Nutritional adjustments often become necessary as other interventions evolve. Changes in activity levels, stress, or body composition may require modifications to macronutrient ratios, meal timing, or supplementation protocols. Regular assessment of nutritional needs ensures continued progress.

Psychological responses to interventions deserve careful attention. Monitoring motivation levels, adherence patterns, and emotional well-being helps identify when adjustments might improve sustainability or effectiveness. Small modifications that enhance consistency often prove more valuable than dramatic changes.

Social support systems impact intervention success and require regular evaluation. Assessing the effectiveness of accountability measures, coaching relationships, and community involvement helps optimize these important support structures.

Technology utilization in monitoring requires periodic review and adjustment. Evaluating the usefulness of various tracking tools and adjusting their implementation helps maintain efficient and effective monitoring systems.

Compliance tracking provides crucial information about intervention feasibility. Regular assessment of adherence patterns helps identify areas where simplification or modification might improve consistency. Practical adjustments that enhance compliance often yield better results than theoretically optimal but challenging protocols.

Cost-benefit analysis of various interventions helps optimize resource allocation. Regular evaluation of time, energy, and financial investments against observed results guides decisions about continuing, modifying, or discontinuing specific approaches.

Integration of multiple interventions requires careful monitoring to prevent overwhelming systems or creating conflicting effects. Regular assessment of how different protocols interact helps maintain synergistic rather than antagonistic relationships between interventions.

Long-term trend analysis reveals patterns that might not be apparent in short-term data. Regular review of extended time periods helps identify gradual changes or cyclical patterns that influence intervention effectiveness.

Flexibility in adjustment strategies maintains intervention effectiveness across changing life circumstances. Having predetermined modification options for various scenarios helps maintain consistency during travel, high-stress periods, or other disruptions.

The art of monitoring and adjusting interventions lies in balancing consistency with adaptation. While stable protocols provide the foundation for progress, thoughtful modifications based on careful monitoring ensure continued effectiveness and optimal results. This dynamic approach to intervention management supports sustainable progress toward health and performance goals.

Progress Tracking

Progress tracking transforms abstract goals into measurable achievements through systematic observation and documentation of change over time. The process of recording and analyzing various metrics provides invaluable feedback that guides future decisions and maintains motivation throughout any optimization journey.

Establishing baseline measurements creates the foundation for meaningful progress tracking. These initial assessments span multiple domains, including physical metrics, performance capabilities, blood markers, and subjective measures of well-being. Without clear starting points, accurately gauging improvement becomes impossible.

Digital tools have revolutionized the way we capture and analyze progress data. Modern applications can track everything from workout performance to sleep patterns, creating comprehensive databases of personal information. However, the key lies not in collecting data for its own sake, but in extracting actionable insights that drive continued improvement.

Photography serves as a powerful progress tracking tool, particularly for physical transformations. Weekly or monthly progress photos, taken under consistent conditions, provide visual evidence of changes that might be difficult to quantify through other means. These visual records often reveal subtle improvements that numbers alone might miss.

Journaling captures qualitative aspects of progress that quantitative measurements cannot adequately represent. Daily or weekly reflections on energy levels, mood, motivation, and general well-being provide context for numerical data and help identify patterns in subjective experience.

Performance metrics require systematic testing protocols to ensure reliable comparison over time. Whether measuring strength, endurance, or skill-based capabilities, consistent testing conditions and methods are crucial for accurate progress assessment. Regular testing intervals help maintain motivation while providing feedback about training effectiveness.

Body composition measurements track changes in muscle mass, fat levels, and overall structure. While scale weight provides one data point, more comprehensive measurements like circumference measurements, skinfold tests, or DEXA scans offer deeper insights into body composition changes.

Blood markers provide objective evidence of internal improvements that might not be immediately apparent through external observations. Regular testing of key health markers helps verify the effectiveness of various interventions and guides necessary adjustments to optimization protocols.

Sleep tracking reveals patterns in recovery quality and quantity over time. Monitoring sleep duration, stages, and efficiency helps optimize rest periods and ensures adequate recovery for continued progress. This data often correlates strongly with performance improvements in other areas.

Habit tracking builds accountability and highlights areas needing attention. Simple checkmarks or scores for daily habits create a clear record of consistency in fundamental behaviors that support larger goals. This basic form of tracking often yields powerful insights about behavior patterns.

Energy levels throughout the day deserve careful monitoring to identify improvements in sustainable performance. Tracking energy patterns helps optimize daily schedules and verify the effectiveness of various interventions aimed at enhancing vitality and productivity.

Cognitive performance tracking measures improvements in mental capabilities over time. Regular assessment of memory, focus, processing speed, and other cognitive functions helps verify the effectiveness of brain optimization strategies.

Stress resilience can be tracked through various markers, including heart rate variability and subjective stress ratings. Monitoring these parameters helps verify improvements in stress management capabilities and guides adjustments to coping strategies.

Nutrition tracking goes beyond simple calorie counting to monitor macro and micronutrient intake patterns. This data helps optimize dietary choices and ensures proper fueling for performance and recovery.

Movement quality assessments track improvements in mobility, stability, and movement efficiency. Regular movement screens help identify areas needing attention and verify progress in movement capability enhancement.

Recovery capacity can be tracked through various markers, including morning heart rate, perceived readiness, and performance metrics. This data helps optimize training frequency and intensity while preventing overreach.

Environmental factors should be recorded alongside progress data to provide context for various measurements. Factors like temperature, humidity, stress levels, and sleep quality can significantly impact performance metrics.

Social connections and support systems deserve tracking attention, as they significantly influence overall well-being and progress. Recording the quality and quantity of social interactions helps optimize this crucial aspect of health.

Long-term trend analysis requires consistent data collection over extended periods. Regular review of these trends helps identify patterns and cycles that might not be apparent in shorter time frames.

The psychological impact of progress tracking cannot be overlooked. Regular review of documented improvements provides powerful motivation during challenging periods and helps maintain commitment to optimization practices.

Success in progress tracking comes from finding the right balance between comprehensive measurement and practical sustainability. While detailed data collection provides valuable insights, the tracking system must remain manageable enough for consistent long-term implementation. The most effective progress tracking systems evolve over time, incorporating new measurements as needed while maintaining focus on the most relevant metrics for current goals.

Long term Maintenance

Long-term maintenance represents the ultimate challenge in any optimization journey, requiring careful attention to sustainability, adaptability, and consistent progression. The key to lasting success lies not in perfect adherence to rigid protocols, but in developing flexible systems that evolve with changing life circumstances while maintaining core principles.

Sustainable practices form the foundation of effective long-term maintenance. Rather than pursuing extreme measures that quickly lead to burnout, focus on establishing habits that can be maintained indefinitely. These foundational behaviors should align with personal values and lifestyle preferences while supporting desired outcomes.

Psychological flexibility plays a crucial role in maintaining progress over extended periods. The ability to adapt to changing circumstances without completely abandoning healthy practices helps prevent the all-or-nothing mindset that often leads to regression. Learning to modify rather than abandon protocols during challenging times maintains momentum.

Regular assessment periods help prevent gradual drift from established practices. Monthly and quarterly reviews provide opportunities to evaluate current habits, identify areas of weakness, and make necessary adjustments before small deviations become significant problems. These checkpoints maintain accountability while allowing for strategic modifications.

Social support systems require ongoing cultivation to maintain their effectiveness over time. Regular connection with like-minded individuals, whether through training partners, health-focused communities, or professional guidance, provides crucial accountability and motivation during challenging periods.

Environmental design supports long-term adherence by making desired behaviors easier to maintain. Creating spaces and systems that naturally encourage healthy choices reduces the daily willpower required to maintain positive habits. This might include home gym setups, organized meal prep areas, or dedicated recovery spaces.

Stress management becomes increasingly important for long-term maintenance as life pressures accumulate. Developing robust coping mechanisms and regular stress-relief practices helps prevent the cascade of negative behaviors that often follows periods of elevated stress.

Recovery protocols must evolve to match changing demands and capabilities. What works during initial optimization phases may become insufficient or excessive as fitness levels and life circumstances change. Regular adjustment of recovery practices ensures continued effectiveness.

Nutritional strategies require periodic updates to match changing activity levels, goals, and physiological needs. Rather than adhering to rigid meal plans, developing flexible eating patterns that can adapt to various situations supports sustainable progress.

Movement practices should emphasize variety and enjoyment to maintain engagement over time. While structured training remains important, incorporating diverse physical activities prevents boredom and supports overall movement capability.

Technology utilization needs regular review to ensure it continues supporting rather than hindering maintenance efforts. Updating tracking systems, adjusting notification settings, and modifying digital tools helps maintain their effectiveness as aids rather than obstacles.

Financial planning plays a crucial role in long-term maintenance. Budgeting for necessary equipment, supplements, professional guidance, and other health-related expenses ensures resources remain available to support ongoing practices.

Sleep optimization requires consistent attention as one of the most fundamental aspects of health maintenance. Regular assessment and adjustment of sleep routines helps maintain this crucial foundation for all other health practices.

Seasonal adjustments acknowledge the natural rhythms that influence health and performance. Modifying protocols to align with changing daylight, weather patterns, and activity levels supports sustainable practice throughout the year.

Professional development often impacts health maintenance strategies. As career demands evolve, health practices must adapt while maintaining their fundamental effectiveness. This might involve adjusting workout timing, meal scheduling, or recovery practices.

Family dynamics significantly influence long-term maintenance success. Integrating health practices with family life, rather than treating them as separate entities, increases sustainability. This might involve family activities, shared meal preparation, or coordinated schedules.

Travel strategies require development for maintaining core practices during disrupted routines. Having predetermined modifications for different travel scenarios helps maintain progress during periods away from normal environments.

Emergency protocols provide clear guidelines for maintaining essential practices during high-stress periods. These simplified versions of regular routines ensure basic health maintenance continues during challenging times.

Documentation systems need regular updates to remain effective tools for long-term tracking. Whether using digital apps or paper journals, ensuring tracking methods remain practical and meaningful supports continued use.

Community engagement offers opportunities for shared learning and motivation. Regular participation in health-focused communities provides inspiration, accountability, and practical strategies for maintaining progress.

The art of long-term maintenance lies in finding the sweet spot between consistency and adaptation. While core principles remain stable, their implementation must evolve with changing circumstances and capabilities. Success comes not from perfect adherence to initial protocols, but from skillful adaptation that maintains forward momentum while accommodating life's natural variations.

Chapter 6: Special Applications

Athletic Performance

Athletic performance represents the pinnacle of human physical capability, combining strength, speed, endurance, and skill into seamless execution. The pursuit of athletic excellence demands a comprehensive approach that integrates multiple facets of training, recovery, and psychological preparation.

Physical preparation forms the cornerstone of athletic development. Structured training programs must balance various fitness components while avoiding the pitfalls of overtraining. Progressive overload principles guide the systematic increase in training demands, allowing the body to adapt and improve without exceeding recovery capabilities.

Movement quality serves as the foundation for all athletic endeavors. Before pursuing maximum performance, athletes must develop proper movement patterns and maintain them under increasingly challenging conditions. This foundation prevents injuries while enabling more effective force production and skill execution.

Speed development requires careful attention to both acceleration and maximum velocity mechanics. Technical drills focusing on proper positioning, force application, and relaxation help athletes maximize their explosive potential. Regular assessment of sprint mechanics ensures continued improvement in this crucial athletic quality.

Strength training plays a vital role in athletic development, extending far beyond mere muscle building. Strategic resistance training enhances force production, reduces injury risk, and improves movement efficiency. Periodized strength programs account for sport-specific demands and competition schedules.

Power development bridges the gap between raw strength and athletic performance. Plyometric training, Olympic lifting variations, and sport-specific power exercises help athletes express their strength rapidly and effectively. Careful progression in power training prevents injury while maximizing adaptation.

Endurance capacity supports both single-effort performance and recovery between repeated efforts. Sport-specific conditioning programs develop the energy systems most relevant to competitive demands. Heart rate monitoring and other metrics guide the intensity and duration of conditioning work.

Agility training enhances an athlete's ability to change direction rapidly while maintaining control. Reactive drills improve decision-making speed while challenging movement capability. Progressive complexity in agility training develops both physical capacity and cognitive processing.

Recovery strategies become increasingly important as training intensity increases. Active recovery sessions, mobility work, and various therapeutic modalities help maintain tissue quality and movement capability.

Regular monitoring of recovery status guides training modifications.

Nutrition for athletic performance requires precise timing and composition of meals. Pre-workout fueling, intra-workout nutrition, and post-exercise recovery nutrition all play crucial roles in supporting training adaptation and performance capability.

Hydration status significantly impacts athletic performance, affecting everything from power output to cognitive function. Individualized hydration protocols account for sweat rates, environmental conditions, and activity demands.

Sleep quality directly influences athletic performance through its effects on recovery, hormone production, and cognitive function. Athletes must prioritize sleep hygiene and maintain consistent sleep schedules to support optimal performance.

Mental preparation distinguishes elite performers from average athletes. Visualization techniques, pre-performance routines, and strategic self-talk enhance competitive execution. Regular practice of mental skills ensures reliability under pressure.

Competition preparation requires careful planning to peak at the right time. Tapering protocols reduce training volume while maintaining intensity, allowing full expression of developed capabilities. Competition-specific preparation includes environmental adaptation and strategic planning.

Skill development continues throughout an athlete's career. Technical refinement through deliberate practice enhances movement efficiency and performance reliability. Video analysis and expert coaching guide ongoing skill improvement.

Team dynamics influence individual athletic performance through various psychological and practical mechanisms. Understanding and optimizing team roles, communication patterns, and collective energy management enhances both individual and group performance.

Environmental adaptation plays a crucial role in performance consistency. Training in various conditions prepares athletes for competition in challenging environments. Heat acclimation, altitude training, and other environmental considerations require specific preparation protocols.

Equipment selection and maintenance significantly impact performance capability. Regular evaluation and adjustment of equipment ensure optimal support for training and competition. Technical specifications must match individual requirements and preferences.

Performance analysis provides crucial feedback for ongoing improvement. Regular testing protocols track progress in various performance metrics. Data analysis guides program adjustments and identifies areas needing additional attention.

Recovery between competitions requires careful management to maintain performance capability throughout a competitive season. Strategic deloading periods and recovery protocols prevent accumulated fatigue while maintaining fitness levels.

The psychology of athletic performance extends beyond basic mental preparation. Understanding motivation, managing pressure, and maintaining focus under various conditions all contribute to consistent execution. Regular practice of psychological skills enhances competitive reliability.

Athletic performance represents a complex interaction of physical capability, technical skill, and psychological readiness. Success requires attention to each component while maintaining their integration into cohesive performance. Continuous refinement of training methods, recovery strategies, and mental preparation techniques supports ongoing development and achievement of athletic potential.

Chronic Disease Management

Chronic disease management requires a comprehensive, personalized approach that addresses both the underlying causes and daily manifestations of ongoing health conditions. Understanding the interconnected nature of chronic conditions allows for more effective intervention strategies and improved quality of life.

Lifestyle modifications form the foundation of successful disease management. Small, consistent changes in daily habits often yield significant improvements in disease progression and symptom management. These modifications must be sustainable and aligned with individual capabilities and preferences.

Nutritional interventions play a crucial role in managing chronic conditions. Anti-inflammatory dietary patterns, blood sugar regulation, and appropriate nutrient timing can significantly impact disease progression. Individual food sensitivities and metabolic responses guide specific dietary recommendations.

Movement protocols must be carefully designed to account for condition-specific limitations while promoting functional improvement. Regular physical activity, appropriately modified for current capabilities, helps maintain mobility and independence while potentially slowing disease progression.

Stress management becomes particularly important in chronic disease contexts, as elevated stress levels often exacerbate symptoms and accelerate decline. Regular practice of stress-reduction techniques helps maintain physiological balance and emotional well-being.

Sleep optimization supports the body's natural healing processes and helps manage inflammation levels. Addressing sleep disturbances through environmental modifications and behavioral interventions improves overall disease management outcomes.

Medication management requires careful attention to timing, interactions, and side effects. Regular review of medication protocols ensures continued effectiveness while minimizing potential complications. Communication with healthcare providers helps optimize pharmaceutical interventions.

Environmental factors significantly influence chronic disease expression. Identifying and modifying environmental triggers helps reduce symptom frequency and severity. This includes attention to air quality, temperature regulation, and exposure to potential irritants.

Social support systems play a vital role in long-term disease management. Building and maintaining supportive relationships helps ensure consistent care while providing emotional reinforcement during challenging periods.

Pain management often requires a multi-modal approach combining pharmaceutical interventions with physical therapy, movement practices, and psychological techniques. Individual response patterns guide the selection and timing of various pain management strategies.

Energy management becomes crucial for maintaining daily function while living with chronic conditions. Strategic pacing of activities and regular rest periods help preserve energy for essential tasks while preventing excessive fatigue.

Regular monitoring of key health markers helps track disease progression and treatment effectiveness. Home monitoring devices and regular professional assessments provide data for adjusting management strategies.

Emotional well-being requires ongoing attention, as chronic conditions often impact mental health. Regular psychological support and emotional regulation practices help maintain resilience and positive outlook.

Preventive measures help minimize acute exacerbations of chronic conditions. Understanding early warning signs and having clear action plans for different scenarios reduces the frequency and severity of disease flares.

Dietary supplementation often supports conventional treatments in managing chronic conditions. Evidence-based supplement protocols, carefully coordinated with existing medications, can help address specific deficiencies and support overall health.

Movement quality assessment guides the development of appropriate exercise modifications. Regular evaluation of functional capabilities helps ensure that physical activity remains both safe and beneficial.

Communication strategies with healthcare providers need regular refinement to ensure effective coordination of care. Clear documentation of symptoms, responses to interventions, and concerns helps optimize treatment approaches.

Daily routine optimization supports consistent implementation of management strategies. Creating sustainable schedules that accommodate both health needs and life responsibilities improves long-term adherence.

Technology utilization can enhance disease management through tracking apps, reminder systems, and monitoring devices. Selecting appropriate tools and integrating them effectively into daily life supports better outcomes.

Emergency preparedness becomes essential for managing unexpected disease exacerbations. Having clear protocols and necessary supplies readily available helps maintain calm and effective response during challenging situations.

Knowledge acquisition about specific conditions and management strategies supports better decision-making and self-advocacy. Staying informed about current research and treatment options while maintaining a critical perspective helps optimize personal care approaches.

Adaptive strategies for various life situations help maintain management consistency during travel, social events, and other disruptions to normal routines. Developing flexible approaches to core management practices supports better long-term outcomes.

The psychological aspects of chronic disease management require ongoing attention. Acceptance, resilience building, and positive coping strategies help maintain emotional well-being while dealing with ongoing health challenges.

Success in chronic disease management comes from finding the right balance between active intervention and acceptance of current limitations. While continuously working to optimize health outcomes, maintaining realistic expectations and appreciating small improvements supports long-term well-being. Regular reassessment and adjustment of management strategies ensures continued effectiveness while accommodating changes in disease progression and life circumstances.

Aging and Longevity

Aging represents a natural biological process that can be significantly influenced by lifestyle choices and environmental factors. The science of longevity extends far beyond mere life extension, focusing on maintaining vitality, cognitive function, and physical capability throughout the aging process.

Cellular health forms the foundation of successful aging. Regular exercise, proper nutrition, and stress management influence cellular repair mechanisms and metabolic efficiency. Research indicates that maintaining optimal cellular function through lifestyle interventions can slow various aspects of biological aging.

Telomere length, a key marker of cellular aging, responds to both positive and negative lifestyle factors. Regular physical activity, stress reduction, and proper sleep habits help preserve telomere length, potentially extending cellular lifespan and reducing age-related decline.

Mitochondrial function plays a crucial role in aging and energy production. Supporting these cellular powerhouses through appropriate exercise, strategic nutrition, and environmental optimization helps maintain energy levels and cellular health throughout the aging process.

Inflammation management becomes increasingly important with age. Chronic inflammation accelerates cellular aging and contributes to various age-related conditions. Anti-inflammatory dietary choices, regular movement, and stress reduction help manage inflammatory processes.

Hormonal balance significantly influences the aging process. Natural hormone optimization through lifestyle interventions supports tissue repair, maintains muscle mass, and preserves cognitive function. Regular monitoring and appropriate interventions help maintain optimal hormonal status.

Brain health requires specific attention during aging. Regular cognitive challenges, social engagement, and physical activity support neuroplasticity and cognitive reserve. Learning new skills and maintaining intellectual curiosity helps preserve mental acuity.

Muscle preservation becomes crucial as age advances. Regular resistance training, adequate protein intake, and proper recovery protocols help maintain muscle mass and functional strength. This preservation of lean tissue supports metabolism and daily function.

Bone density maintenance requires ongoing attention to prevent age-related deterioration. Weight-bearing exercise, proper nutrition, and hormone balance support skeletal health. Regular assessment helps track and maintain bone strength.

Joint health significantly impacts quality of life during aging. Maintaining appropriate movement patterns, managing inflammation, and supporting tissue repair helps preserve joint function and mobility.

Cardiovascular health remains paramount throughout the aging process. Regular aerobic activity, stress management, and proper nutrition support heart function and circulation. Monitoring cardiovascular markers helps guide intervention strategies.

Sleep quality often changes with age but remains crucial for health maintenance. Optimizing sleep environment, maintaining consistent schedules, and addressing age-related sleep disruptions supports overall well-being.

Digestive function requires specific attention during aging. Supporting gut health through appropriate fiber intake, probiotic-rich foods, and stress management helps maintain nutrient absorption and immune function.

Social connections play a vital role in healthy aging. Maintaining strong relationships and community involvement supports both psychological well-being and cognitive function. Regular social interaction provides emotional support and mental stimulation.

Stress resilience becomes increasingly important as age advances. Developing effective coping mechanisms and maintaining regular stress-reduction practices helps preserve both physical and mental health.

Environmental factors significantly influence the aging process. Minimizing exposure to toxins, maintaining appropriate light exposure, and creating supportive living spaces helps optimize health outcomes.

Nutritional needs evolve with age, requiring careful attention to both macro and micronutrient intake. Focusing on nutrient-dense foods while maintaining appropriate caloric balance supports healthy aging.

Movement patterns require regular assessment and modification to accommodate changing capabilities. Maintaining functional movement while respecting current limitations helps preserve independence and physical capability.

Recovery capacity often decreases with age, necessitating careful attention to exercise intensity and frequency. Proper balance between activity and rest supports continued physical improvement while preventing overtraining.

Preventive health measures become increasingly important with age. Regular health screenings, appropriate medical care, and proactive lifestyle interventions help identify and address potential issues early.

Vision and hearing preservation requires specific attention during aging. Regular assessment and appropriate protective measures help maintain sensory function and quality of life.

Skin health reflects both internal and external aging processes. Proper nutrition, sun protection, and appropriate skincare support both function and appearance of aging skin.

The psychological aspects of aging require careful attention. Maintaining a positive outlook while realistically addressing age-related changes supports emotional well-being and life satisfaction.

Successful aging involves embracing change while actively working to maintain health and function. Rather than fighting against natural processes, focus on optimizing current capabilities while building resilience for future challenges. Regular assessment and adjustment of health practices ensures continued effectiveness while accommodating changing needs and capabilities throughout the aging process.

Chapter 7: Future Perspectives

Emerging Research

Scientific discovery continues to reshape our understanding of human health and performance, with groundbreaking research emerging across multiple disciplines. Recent studies have unveiled fascinating insights into cellular regeneration, metabolic optimization, and cognitive enhancement that promise to revolutionize healthcare approaches.

Epigenetic research has revealed remarkable plasticity in gene expression, demonstrating how lifestyle choices directly influence genetic activity. Studies show that exercise, nutrition, and stress management can alter gene expression patterns within hours, supporting the notion that our daily choices significantly impact our genetic destiny.

Microbiome studies have expanded dramatically, uncovering intricate connections between gut bacteria and various aspects of health. New research indicates that gut flora influences everything from immune function to mental health, suggesting targeted interventions could treat numerous conditions through microbiome modification.

Chronobiology research has highlighted the crucial role of circadian rhythms in health optimization. Studies demonstrate that timing of activities, from eating to exercise, significantly impacts their effectiveness. Understanding these biological rhythms helps maximize the benefits of various health interventions.

Neuroplasticity research continues to challenge previous assumptions about brain development and recovery. Recent findings suggest that the brain maintains significant adaptive capacity throughout life, with appropriate stimulation and support potentially enhancing cognitive function at any age.

Mitochondrial function studies have revealed new approaches to energy production and cellular health. Research indicates that specific exercise protocols and nutritional interventions can enhance mitochondrial density and efficiency, potentially improving energy levels and longevity.

Inflammation research has identified novel pathways and intervention strategies. Studies show that chronic inflammation underlies many modern health challenges, while also revealing new methods for managing inflammatory responses through lifestyle and therapeutic approaches.

Stem cell research has progressed significantly, showing promise for tissue regeneration and healing. Studies demonstrate that certain lifestyle factors can enhance natural stem cell production and function, suggesting new approaches to tissue repair and maintenance.

Sleep science has unveiled crucial mechanisms linking rest quality to health outcomes. Research highlights how different sleep stages influence recovery, learning, and cellular repair, emphasizing the importance of optimizing sleep architecture.

Muscle physiology research has revealed new insights into strength development and maintenance. Studies show that resistance training creates more complex adaptations than previously understood, involving both mechanical and hormonal responses.

Cardiovascular research has identified novel markers for heart health and disease prevention. Studies demonstrate that traditional risk factors tell only part of the story, with new indicators providing earlier warning signs of potential issues.

Cognitive science has expanded our understanding of learning and memory formation. Research reveals that skill acquisition involves more complex neural adaptations than previously thought, suggesting new approaches to training and education.

Nutritional science continues to evolve, with studies revealing intricate relationships between food timing, composition, and health outcomes. Research shows that individual responses to different dietary patterns vary significantly, supporting personalized nutrition approaches.

Exercise physiology research has uncovered new mechanisms of adaptation and recovery. Studies demonstrate that training responses involve complex interactions between multiple systems, requiring more nuanced approaches to program design.

Stress research has identified novel pathways through which psychological states influence physical health. Studies show that mental stress creates measurable changes in cellular function, highlighting the importance of comprehensive stress management.

Aging research has revealed previously unknown mechanisms of cellular senescence and repair. Studies suggest that certain interventions might slow or partially reverse aspects of biological aging, opening new possibilities for health span extension.

Environmental health studies have demonstrated how various exposures influence genetic expression and health outcomes. Research indicates that managing environmental factors plays a crucial role in health optimization and disease prevention.

Recovery science has expanded our understanding of adaptation and supercompensation. Studies show that optimal recovery involves more complex processes than previously recognized, requiring careful attention to multiple factors.

Hormone research has revealed intricate feedback loops and regulatory mechanisms. Studies demonstrate that hormonal balance influences health more substantially than previously understood, affecting everything from mood to physical performance.

Brain-gut connection studies have uncovered bidirectional communication pathways affecting both mental and physical health. Research shows that this axis plays a crucial role in immune function, mood regulation, and overall well-being.

Technological advances continue to provide new insights into human biology and health optimization. Wearable devices and sophisticated monitoring systems offer unprecedented ability to track and analyze various health markers in real-time.

Future research directions promise even more exciting discoveries in understanding human health and performance. Ongoing studies in genetics, neuroscience, and cellular biology suggest that current knowledge represents just the beginning of potential breakthroughs in health optimization and disease prevention.

The rapid pace of scientific discovery necessitates regular updates to health and performance protocols. Staying informed about emerging research while maintaining a critical perspective helps integrate new findings into existing practice. This dynamic field continues to evolve, offering increasingly sophisticated approaches to human health optimization.

Technology Integration

Modern health optimization increasingly relies on sophisticated technological tools that enhance monitoring, analysis, and intervention strategies. The integration of technology into health practices has revolutionized our ability to track progress, identify patterns, and implement targeted interventions with unprecedented precision.

Wearable devices have evolved far beyond simple step counters, now offering continuous monitoring of various physiological parameters. Heart rate variability, sleep patterns, and activity levels can be tracked throughout the day, providing valuable insights into recovery status and overall health trends. These devices help identify optimal training windows and recovery needs based on real-time physiological data.

Mobile applications have become powerful tools for health management, offering everything from workout guidance to nutrition tracking. These platforms can analyze eating patterns, suggest meal modifications, and even predict potential nutrient deficiencies based on logged food intake. Integration between different apps allows for comprehensive health data analysis, revealing connections between various lifestyle factors and health outcomes.

Smart home technology contributes significantly to health optimization through environmental control. Automated lighting systems can support natural circadian rhythms, while air quality monitors help maintain optimal breathing conditions. Temperature regulation and humidity control systems further enhance recovery and sleep quality.

Virtual coaching platforms provide personalized guidance through algorithm-based analysis of individual data. These systems can adjust workout recommendations based on recovery status, suggest nutrition modifications according to activity levels, and offer real-time feedback on movement patterns during exercise.

Genetic testing technology offers insights into individual predispositions and potential response patterns to various interventions. This information helps customize nutrition, exercise, and recovery protocols to align with genetic factors, potentially improving intervention effectiveness.

Blood glucose monitors provide continuous data on metabolic responses to different foods and activities. This immediate feedback helps optimize meal timing and composition while identifying individual glucose triggers and patterns.

Movement analysis systems utilize camera technology and sensors to assess exercise form and movement quality. These tools provide immediate feedback on technique, helping prevent injuries and optimize training effectiveness.

Sleep tracking technology has advanced significantly, now offering detailed analysis of sleep architecture and quality. These systems can identify disruption patterns, suggest environmental modifications, and help optimize sleep timing based on individual circadian rhythms.

Heart rate monitoring technology provides continuous cardiovascular data during both activity and rest. This information helps guide exercise intensity, monitor recovery status, and track overall cardiovascular health trends.

Strength training technology incorporates velocity-based measurements and force production analysis. These tools help optimize resistance training by providing immediate feedback on movement quality and power output.

Hydration monitoring systems track fluid balance through various physiological markers. This technology helps maintain optimal hydration status by providing customized intake recommendations based on activity levels and environmental conditions.

Recovery technology includes various tools for monitoring and enhancing the restoration process. From compression systems to electromagnetic therapy devices, these technologies support tissue repair and maintenance.

Nutrition analysis technology has evolved to include detailed nutrient tracking and meal planning capabilities. These systems can identify potential deficiencies, suggest modifications, and even generate shopping lists based on nutritional goals.

Environmental monitoring technology helps optimize living and training spaces. From air quality sensors to EMF meters, these tools help create healthier environments for both recovery and performance.

Stress monitoring systems track various markers of psychological and physiological stress. This information helps identify triggers and patterns while guiding stress management interventions.

Communication platforms facilitate better coordination between health practitioners and clients. Secure messaging systems and data sharing capabilities enhance care continuity and intervention effectiveness.

Data analysis platforms integrate information from multiple sources to identify patterns and trends. These systems help optimize intervention timing and selection while tracking progress toward health goals.

Virtual reality technology offers new approaches to movement training and stress management. Immersive environments can enhance exercise engagement while providing novel ways to practice relaxation techniques.

Biofeedback devices provide real-time information about various physiological processes. This immediate feedback helps develop better control over different aspects of physical and mental function.

The successful integration of health technology requires careful consideration of individual needs and preferences. While these tools offer powerful capabilities, their effectiveness depends on appropriate selection and consistent use. Regular evaluation of technology utilization helps ensure that chosen tools continue to support health goals effectively.

Privacy considerations remain crucial when implementing health technology. Careful attention to data security and sharing settings helps protect sensitive information while maintaining the benefits of technological integration.

The future of health technology continues to evolve rapidly, with new tools and capabilities emerging regularly. Maintaining a balanced approach to technology adoption, focusing on tools that provide meaningful benefits while avoiding unnecessary complexity, supports sustainable health optimization practices.

Personalized Medicine

Medicine is undergoing a profound transformation from a one-size-fits-all approach to highly individualized care protocols based on unique genetic, environmental, and lifestyle factors. This revolutionary shift enables healthcare practitioners to develop targeted interventions that consider each person's distinct biological makeup and life circumstances.

Genetic testing has emerged as a cornerstone of personalized medicine, providing insights into individual disease risks, medication responses, and optimal intervention strategies. By analyzing specific genetic markers, practitioners can identify potential health challenges before they manifest and implement preventive measures tailored to genetic predispositions.

Metabolic profiling reveals individual variations in how the body processes nutrients, medications, and environmental compounds. These insights allow for precise adjustments to nutrition plans and supplement protocols, optimizing therapeutic outcomes through personalized interventions.

Hormonal assessment has evolved beyond simple reference ranges to consider individual baseline patterns and optimal functional levels. This nuanced approach enables practitioners to develop hormone optimization strategies that account for unique biological rhythms and requirements.

Microbiome analysis provides crucial information about individual gut flora composition and function. Understanding these personal bacterial patterns helps guide specific dietary modifications and probiotic interventions to support optimal digestive and immune function.

Environmental sensitivity testing identifies individual reactions to various compounds and exposures. This information helps create personalized environmental modification strategies to minimize negative impacts while optimizing beneficial exposures.

Nutrigenomics combines genetic information with nutritional science to develop highly targeted dietary recommendations. This approach considers how individual genetic variations influence nutrient requirements and food responses, enabling precise nutritional optimization.

Pharmacogenetics examines how genetic variations affect medication metabolism and effectiveness. This knowledge allows practitioners to select and dose medications more effectively, reducing adverse reactions while improving therapeutic outcomes.

Immune system profiling helps identify individual susceptibilities and response patterns. This information guides the development of personalized immune support protocols and infection prevention strategies.

Cardiovascular risk assessment has expanded to include advanced markers and individual response patterns. This comprehensive approach enables more precise prevention strategies and targeted interventions for heart health optimization.

Sleep pattern analysis reveals individual circadian rhythms and rest requirements. Understanding these personal patterns helps optimize sleep timing and environmental conditions for maximum recovery benefit.

Exercise response profiling identifies how individuals adapt to different types of physical activity. This information guides the development of personalized training programs that maximize benefits while minimizing injury risk.

Stress response patterns vary significantly between individuals, requiring personalized management strategies. Understanding individual stress triggers and response mechanisms helps develop targeted coping protocols.

Cognitive function assessment considers personal learning patterns and neurological variations. This information enables the development of targeted strategies for maintaining and enhancing mental performance.

Aging rate analysis examines individual biological aging patterns through various biomarkers. This information helps guide personalized interventions to optimize health span and maintain functionality.

Detoxification capacity testing reveals individual variations in processing and eliminating environmental toxins. Understanding these patterns helps develop targeted support protocols for optimal cellular health.

Inflammatory response profiling identifies personal triggers and patterns of inflammation. This knowledge enables more precise intervention strategies for managing chronic inflammatory conditions.

Recovery capacity assessment examines individual restoration patterns and requirements. This information guides the development of personalized recovery protocols that optimize adaptation and performance.

Nutritional absorption testing reveals individual variations in nutrient processing and utilization. Understanding these patterns helps optimize supplement protocols and dietary choices for maximum benefit.

Energy system analysis examines personal patterns of energy production and utilization. This information guides the development of targeted interventions to optimize cellular energy production.

The implementation of personalized medicine requires ongoing monitoring and adjustment of interventions based on individual responses. Regular assessment of various biomarkers helps track progress and modify protocols as needed for optimal outcomes.

Successful personalized medicine depends on active patient participation and understanding. Education about individual patterns and response mechanisms helps ensure better compliance with personalized protocols.

The future of personalized medicine continues to evolve as new testing methods and intervention strategies emerge. Maintaining flexibility in treatment approaches while incorporating new evidence-based practices ensures optimal care delivery.

The integration of multiple data points creates a comprehensive picture of individual health patterns and needs. This holistic approach enables more effective intervention strategies by addressing root causes rather than isolated symptoms.

The ultimate goal of personalized medicine is to optimize health outcomes through precisely targeted interventions based on individual characteristics. This approach represents a significant advancement in healthcare delivery, offering improved effectiveness and reduced side effects compared to standardized protocols.

Public Health Applications

Public health initiatives have evolved significantly, incorporating advanced understanding of population health dynamics while maintaining focus on individual well-being. These programs now extend beyond traditional disease prevention to encompass comprehensive health optimization strategies for entire communities.

Community-based wellness programs have demonstrated remarkable success in promoting healthy lifestyle habits. Local initiatives that combine education, access to resources, and social support create sustainable behavior changes across diverse populations. These programs often start with simple interventions, such as walking groups or cooking classes, which gradually expand into comprehensive health promotion networks.

Workplace health programs have transformed corporate environments into centers for health optimization. Companies implementing comprehensive wellness initiatives report significant improvements in employee health markers, productivity, and job satisfaction. These programs typically include ergonomic improvements, stress management resources, and opportunities for physical activity during work hours.

School-based health initiatives play a crucial role in establishing lifelong wellness habits. Programs that integrate nutrition education, physical activity, and stress management techniques into daily curricula show promising results in improving student health outcomes. These early interventions create foundations for lifetime health awareness and positive behaviors.

Urban planning has embraced health-conscious design principles, creating environments that naturally promote physical activity and social interaction. Cities incorporating green spaces, walking paths, and community gardens report improved public health metrics across all age groups. These architectural and planning decisions support natural movement patterns and healthy lifestyle choices.

Environmental health programs address the crucial connection between ecosystem and human health. Initiatives focusing on air quality improvement, water safety, and reduced toxic exposures demonstrate significant positive impacts on community health outcomes. These programs often combine regulatory measures with public education campaigns.

Food security programs have expanded beyond basic nutrition to embrace comprehensive health optimization principles. Community gardens, farmers' markets, and educational programs about whole food preparation help ensure access to quality nutrition while building valuable life skills.

Mental health support systems have evolved to include preventive measures and early intervention strategies. Community-based programs that reduce stigma and provide accessible resources show promising results in improving population mental health outcomes. These initiatives often integrate traditional counseling with modern stress management techniques.

Senior health programs focus on maintaining independence and quality of life through active aging initiatives. Community centers offering social interaction, physical activity, and cognitive stimulation help older adults maintain health and functionality longer. These programs often include intergenerational activities that benefit both seniors and younger participants.

Youth sports programs have expanded to emphasize long-term health development rather than just competitive success. These initiatives now include injury prevention education, proper nutrition guidance, and stress management techniques, creating comprehensive approaches to youth wellness.

Public health education campaigns utilize modern communication channels to reach diverse populations effectively. Social media platforms, mobile applications, and community networks help disseminate accurate health information and practical wellness strategies. These campaigns often include interactive elements that encourage active participation.

Emergency preparedness programs now incorporate health optimization principles alongside traditional response protocols. Communities with well-developed preparation systems show better health outcomes during and after crisis situations. These programs emphasize both physical and psychological resilience.

Occupational health initiatives extend beyond basic safety measures to include comprehensive wellness support. Programs addressing ergonomics, stress management, and work-life balance show significant benefits for both employees and organizations. These initiatives often include regular health screenings and preventive care measures.

Community fitness programs provide accessible physical activity options for diverse populations. Public spaces equipped with exercise stations, organized group activities, and professional guidance help overcome common barriers to regular exercise. These programs often adapt to serve various fitness levels and abilities.

Nutrition support programs combine education with practical resources for healthy eating. Community kitchens, cooking classes, and meal planning workshops help translate nutritional knowledge into daily practices. These initiatives often include cultural considerations to ensure broader acceptance and implementation.

www.ingramcontent.com/pod-product-compliance
Lightning Source LLC
Chambersburg PA
CBHW050536160726
48003CB00002B/622